THE GRIEVING INDIAN

Arthur H.

with George McPeek

Indian Life Books

Intertribal Christian Communications (Canada) Inc.
P.O. Box 3765 Station B
Winnipeg, Manitoba R2W 3R6
Canada

The Grieving Indian

by Arthur H.

with George McPeek

Copyright © 1988 by
Intertribal Christian Communications (Canada) Inc.

Second Printing, November 1988

Unless otherwise marked, all scripture quotations are from *Holy Bible, New Life
Version*, published by Christian Literature International, Canby, Oregon.
Used by permission.

Quotations from the Twelve Steps of the AA program are reprinted here with
the permission of Alcoholics Anonymous World Services Inc. The opinions
expressed in this book are those of the author and in no way reflect the
endorsement of AA.

The publishers wish to thank the following companies for permission to quote
from their publications: Abingdon, the publishers of *The Many Faces of Grief*
and *Understanding Grief* by Edgar N. Jackson; Random House, the publishers
of *Help For Your Grief* by Arthur Freese; Harper and Row Publishers,
publishers of *The Violence Within* by Paul Tournier.

The names of people in this book, and the details of their stories,
have been changed to protect their privacy.

Cover art and design by Don Monkman

ISBN 0-920379-07-9

Printed in Canada

TABLE OF CONTENTS

Preface

VAST NUMBERS OF our native people are so weighed down with problems that they are close to self-destruction. **The Grieving Indian** is my small effort to address these problems. In these pages, I offer some practical suggestions gathered from many years as a clergyman, an alcoholic, and a counselor for the chemically dependent.

As a young minister not yet thirty, my efforts to encourage my native congregation to be more responsible, dependable believers were frustrating. Further frustration followed when I relapsed back into alcoholism and struggled for the next twenty years as I tried desperately to regain the spiritual ground I had somehow lost. I attempted many "new starts," but they would only last for three or four months and I'd be back to drinking again. I wanted to be different, but nothing I tried ever worked. Many years later, through the courage of my wife, to whom this book is dedicated, the grace of God and the disciplines of the AA program, I finally found sobriety. Then, after training, I became a counselor in Indian alcohol treatment centers.

Over the years, as I listened to close to two thousand native patients share their inner problems and hurts, I began to see a pattern. Almost everyone was bothered by the same two problems—unfinished grieving and separation from their parents during childhood or early teenage years. They were also having difficulty with alcohol and drug addiction, but these seemed to be an attempt to escape the pain of other very deep, emotional hurts. During these years, I came to understand that until both the emotional and the addiction problems are dealt with, even most of those who are converted to Christ are going to suffer relapses indefinitely.

While this book is mainly directed towards my native people, it also has a message for the Christian church. There must be a better way for us to help alcoholics, who are so often turned off by religion. I think this is largely because of the attitude of many church members toward those with chemical dependency problems. Many consider the alcoholic to be beyond help. Such attitudes hinder the church greatly and must be changed. If God is able to deliver those bound by lust, selfishness and hate, He can also release those who are enslaved by alcoholism. My own life is living proof.

Until this attitude problem is cleared up, I believe that Alcoholics Anonymous (AA), or some similar program, is a necessary bridge between the church and alcoholics. I believe that recovering alcoholics who are Christians should remain in the AA program in order to witness to other alcoholics of their faith in Christ. Those who do not know the Lord will have to start with "God as they understand Him." Then once they have adequately dealt with their alcohol addiction, perhaps they will be open to genuine spiritual experience and biblical teaching.

Someone has said if we do not deal with the spirit world, it will deal with us. This is also true of problems with deep inner hurts and addiction. If we do not deal with them, they will deal with us. Every Christian worker and counselor who does not use the available community resources will continue to watch helplessly as addiction and unresolved grieving take their toll on human lives. To bring this tragic waste to an end, counselors and alcoholics alike must be willing to accept the help that is available.

My hope and prayer for this book is that it will be used to bring an end to the grieving of our Indian people and to help free them to fulfil the great potential which they all possess.

Arthur H., 1988

Foreword

ART H. HAS been my friend for more than thirty years. During half that time, Art was drinking. As difficult as those years were—for both Art and his friends—they were the years that taught him the heartbreaking lessons that lend credibility to his present counseling ministry and to this book.

Now, having acquired chemical-dependency counseling credentials, and having counseled in Indian and non-Indian programs for twelve years, Art can address the dependency trauma both from a clinical and experiential foundation. Once Art was a practicing dependent. Now he is a recovering alcoholic, a man well acquainted with grief.

Art's grief seminars have been presented to Indian people, non-Indians, and to persons of both groups who work with the chemically dependent. Art's workshops demonstrate that he has a firm grip on the central issues involved. He has been there. But Art not only identifies the problem, he proposes practical, biblical solutions.

The statistics grip all of us, for they graph the sources of grief among Indian people. Art reviews these tragic causes, and he prescribes spiritual healing founded on biblical principles that led him back to wholeness.

This book will be helpful to all who grieve, for it speaks to hearts caught up in grief from the heart of one who has been there. **The Grieving Indian** will be a valuable tool in the hands of all who care.

Art's ability to articulate the problem and communicate hope surpasses anything I have thus far heard or read. It is my prayer that this book will bring that hope to many as they struggle toward the resolution of grief.

Wally Olson
Coordinator, Indian Ministries Advisory Committee
Baptist General Conference
Minnesota Baptist Conference

CHAPTER ONE

A Promise Made

MY OJIBWE INDIAN name is Shingwauk, which means "a tall white pine," but I have not always lived up to this name. There were many years when mine was a sick and shattered world. My life was totally broken to pieces. In those days, I stood tall only in body. My soul was mired in the deadly depths of alcoholism and spiritual deadness. It is only by the grace of God and the wise actions of a loving wife that I am alive today. Because they stepped in, I was spared from being another Indian statistic. Without them, I would have died the victim of acute alcoholism, brought on in part by the lingering effects of grief over a neglected childhood.

The Grieving Indian is the story of my brokenness, and beyond that, the brokenness of my Indian people. But it is also a story of help and hope. Read it with an open mind and a tender heart. Let me share the painful lessons I have learned, and then perhaps together, we can help our Indian brothers and sisters bring their grieving to an end.

I am an American Indian, enrolled in the agency at Ashland, Wisconsin. My family and I were members of the St. Croix Band, sometimes referred to as the "Lost Tribe" because we had no reservation. This had a strong effect on us. For one thing, without a land-base to call home, we found ourselves moving around a great deal. Over the years, we lived in a number of different towns for periods ranging from several months to three or four years. Having no reservation home also meant no financial help, which most Indians normally receive. Trying to make ends meet, we left Wisconsin in 1940 and migrated into Minnesota to work in the woods. I have been a Minnesotan ever since.

Ours was a hand-to-mouth existence. We lived in poverty. Each spring, we were given a fishing line, hooks and sinkers which were to last for the season. The fish we caught were our main source of food, along with what squirrels we were able to kill with slingshots.

One day when I was six years old, my mother packed several of us children up. She then took us down to the railroad station and put us on the train. Ma gave us a basket of food and told us we were going on a picnic. After talking real friendly to the conductor and telling us to behave, she waved goodbye. It sounded like fun, so we left in high spirits.

We rode for what seemed like a very long time, before the conductor finally came by. He opened up the picnic basket and told us to eat. After a while, we came to a large city and were moved to another train. By this time I was tired of our adventure. I hoped this train would take us home, but it didn't. Instead, it took us on down to the Federal Government Indian School at Tomah, Wisconsin. We were there for three years without seeing our parents. Then after a brief time at home one summer, we spent another three years away at Indian schools. The timing of this separation could not have been worse. Right during the time from ages six to twelve, when we were shaping our values and our conscience and really needed them, our parents were not there to give us their support.

When we finally returned home to stay after six years away at school, we found our mother had divorced our dad and was already re-married. We heard there was some sort of problem, but we really did not understand what it was all about until we saw the new man in our home. It was a shattering experience that soon got worse.

We were only home for a short while when we found we could not get along with our step-father and were forced to move to our grandmother's place. This meant that not only was our dad gone, but so was our home. We were never to live with our mother again after that, except for brief visits.

Grandmother welcomed us to her home and that is where we stayed until we were old enough to leave. Our basic needs were met except for one thing—the necessary correction and influence of parents. This made us double losers. We missed out on our parents' input as children, and we missed out again during the difficult teenage years. Between living with our grandparents and staying in homes of farmers where we would work for our board through the summer months, we were raised without any kind of parental guidance. There was no one to help us with the structure of our conscience or in the development of any kind of spiritual values by which to live. As a result, a few of my cousins, my brothers and I became some of the biggest thieves in the two-county area surrounding our home. Fortunately for me, I was never sent off to one of the reformatories as most of the rest of them were.

During these years, we had no communication with our father. We really did not know where he was or what he was doing. We only saw him on the rare occasion when he came out of the woods to visit his parents. He would be there for perhaps a week and then suddenly one day he would be gone again, and we would not see him for another six months or perhaps a year. I respected my dad and loved him. Even though he drank periodically when he came out of the woods, he still had a lot of good characteristics.

I was introduced to alcohol at a very early age. My mother made home brew and sold it. This was the way she made a living for us, and so there was always a lot of drinking going on in the home while we were there.

Later, when I was at my grandparents, my father also introduced me to hard liquor. He bought moonshine (illegal) whiskey by the gallon on some occasions and would pour it into a lot of pint bottles. Then he stashed these around under haystacks and brush piles in the community. On one occasion while we were walking over to visit a neighbor, he gave me a pint. I was not sure what he wanted me to do with it, so I just carried it. After a while, he asked me why I wasn't drinking. Then as if to show me how it was done, he pulled out his bottle and took several big gulps. Following his example, I lifted my bottle and did the same. This was the pattern that was set for me.

When I was a teenager, the U.S. Army began testing the war-time use of planes for bombing enemy targets. From the day I heard about it, I wanted to be involved. But it wasn't flying planes that caught my interest; I wanted to be the bombardier who dropped the bombs that could destroy.

At the time, I was not aware of a build-up of anger inside me, but looking back I can see it was there. I resented my mother for divorcing my dad and also for remarrying. I resented the two stepfathers that followed. I also was very bitter towards mother for sending us off to the government school and for the manner in which she did it. I resented the schools, the teachers, the government and especially the Bureau of Indian Affairs. I am sure now that all this rage gave rise to my growing desire to be a bombardier. It was one way I could strike back at the world for all the hurts I had suffered.

World War II brought further separation to our family. I was drafted in 1943. The government asked me to choose which branch of the service I wanted to join, and I picked the Army Air Corps. I figured this was my chance to fulfill my boyhood dream of being a bombardier, but they turned me down because of my weight and height. Instead they sent me to Georgia for training in communications. I learned to work with teletype machines and later became a control tower operator.

In December 1943 we left for twenty-eight months of service in North Africa, on the island of Corsica and in Italy. From the start we found ourselves actively engaged in war. I was on tower control duty on many of the mornings when our B-25 bombers took off. As I gave them clearance and watched them taxi out and line up for takeoff, my gut was filled with a jungle of mixed emotions. I envied those men and the wings they wore. I would have done almost anything to be one of them. And I hated myself for being too big for combat duty as a bombardier. My whole tour of duty was turning into a major disappointment.

As the days and weeks went by, my job in the control tower fanned the flame of my desire to be a bombardier. I longed to be in the air where the action was. My body and soul remained on duty in the tower, but in spirit I was with our squadron. I followed their progress through whatever radio transmission I could pick up. At times, bits and pieces of their conversation came in, especially when they were under attack from enemy fighters. Then, when silence followed, it was almost unbearable. Were they hit or did they get away?

It was always a relief when at last the returning planes made contact. We quickly cleared the field for their landing. Fire trucks and ambulances lined up along the runway ready for action. Then suddenly the B-25s were back. Those carrying wounded men came directly in, while the rest circled the air strip. I counted those planes. And I followed with my eyes as the ambulances raced away to the group medical facilities.

When that day's shift ended, my first stop was the squadron bulletin board. I studied the bomb strikes that had just been made. Then I looked up the crew members who had gone on the mission to hear about it first hand. What happened when the radio was silent? How many fighters attacked them? How many did they hit? Did they get any help from our own fighter support?

At last, when the questions were all asked and answered, I returned to my tent. We had made it through that raid, but I knew another one was coming tomorrow.

As the war progressed, we lost many bombardiers, and a call went out for anyone wishing to volunteer for flight duty. I jumped at the chance. After passing the test, I was summoned to Cape Bon in Tunisia for three months of training. I was then assigned to a bomber crew. My buddies thought it was good luck to have an Indian on their team, but I felt I was the lucky one. At long last, I was a bombardier.

I went into my new mission feeling pretty brave. We were supposed to wear protective gear and a helmet, but I figured I didn't need it. Then, our plane got hit, and I changed my mind in a hurry. These were not the pleasure trips I thought they would be, and I started wearing every kind of protection they gave us.

On about our twenty-fifth bombing mission, we had a particularly rough time. We lost two of our six planes and the rest got shot up pretty badly. I was wounded, but we made it back to the air strip. It was at this point that I felt luck had deserted me and for the first time a real fear set in. It is still vivid in my mind today. From then on, each mission was a battle with terror, but I still stuck with it. I suppose it was my boyhood dream that kept me there.

After one mission where we missed our target, our commander told us we were going to keep going back until we got it. As we left the briefing room, I knew I was not able to handle the fear that was welling up inside me. As soon as I had changed into my street clothes, I headed for a nearby village and began to drink with a vengeance. I ended up so thoroughly drunk I do not remember how I got home. The rest of my tour of duty followed this same pattern. I could not handle my fear unless I spent almost all my time on the ground drinking. I would sober up just enough to be able to fly the next day, then as soon as we landed, I would be back at the booze. This went on day after day and resulted in me becoming a confirmed, chronic alcoholic.

There were a lot of desperation prayers during those days of terror. I did not know for sure if God existed, but in case He did, I pleaded with Him to bring me home safely from those bombing raids. If He held up

His end of the bargain, I promised I would be anything He wanted me to be, even a preacher. That was a real concession on my part. My brother, Frank, was a minister and I thought that was the lowest job on the totem pole, but I was desperate. I prayed like this each time we headed toward our targets on the rest of the seventy missions we flew. By the time the war was over, these promises were very real to me, but so was alcohol's hold on my life. The day I got out of the army, I was so drunk I couldn't even sign my discharge papers.

When I was released in June 1945, I returned to Superior, Wisconsin to do what I knew best—drink. For the next year, I went from one drinking party to another, celebrating with friends and relatives who were also just getting out of the service. I knew I had made promises to God, but for the moment I was marching to the orders of alcohol.

CHAPTER TWO

A Promise Kept

ONE DAY TOWARDS the end of my first year back from service, my brother Frank came to visit. He was a minister, and when he invited me to spend a week with him, I was not too excited. There was a lot of partying going on at the time, and I did not want to miss it. But Frank would not take no for an answer. He kept after me until I finally agreed to visit in his home for a week.

Shortly after that, on January 19, 1947, I came face to face with the promises I made to God during the war. Frank invited me to attend one of the prayer meetings in his church, so I went along. That evening, he came over and asked whether I had ever considered giving my heart to the Lord Jesus Christ and if I would be ready to do that.

Right away I remembered my prayers of desperation during the war. "I'll do whatever You want me to do, if You will just bring me home safely," I had promised. Now here I was safe and in one piece, and God was coming to collect.

I looked at Frank and nodded "yes." God had kept His end of the bargain, and it was time I kept mine. I thought being a Christian was part of my war-time contract, sort of a gentleman's agreement. And so, I made my decision to become a Christian that night.

Not long after that, I felt God calling me into the ministry. I did not want to do it, but I felt thoroughly convinced that this deep impression and vision was definitely from the Lord. That is when I began to make preparation to go into the ministry. I did not have any money, but fortunately I was eligible for four years of training because of my time in the service. In the fall of 1947, I enrolled at the North Central Bible Institute in

Minneapolis and began my studies.

I was only in school a few months when a group of Christian Indians contacted me. They invited me to join their part-time ministry to native people in Wisconsin and Minnesota. They were also interested in outreach to the Sioux settlements of Prairie Island and Granite Falls south of Minneapolis. I accepted their offer and began my preaching among these people that same year.

The second year at Bible school, I was married and we started our family. I was also able to land a good, part-time job at the Medical Arts Building in Minneapolis. One day in 1949, I came to work with a severe head and chest cold. I felt so miserable that I asked if I could go home.

Instead of saying "yes," the pharmacist took me back into the stock room. He poured half a glass of something from one of the large containers and handed it to me. "Drink this, then wait back here for about twenty minutes," he said.

I did what I was told and was surprised at how well I felt. I was soon able to go about my work and finish off the shift.

The next day, I was back to feeling the same way, and so once again I was given another half-glass of this liquid. In no time at all, I was feeling much better and was able to do my work.

A month later, when I was suffering with another cold, I asked the head pharmacist if he could give me a bottle of this cough medicine to take home, which he did. This is how I began to medicate myself whenever I felt a cold coming on. Over the years that followed, I drank many a gallon of this medication. Unfortunately, I neglected to read the contents listed on the label. My "miracle" medicine was terpin hydrate and codeine, a very potent cough syrup. It contained 42.5 percent alcohol, which, by liquor standards, was 85-proof, about the same as whiskey.

This was how I was brought back into contact with

alcohol. At the time, I had no idea I was an alcoholic, so the problem went untreated. In the years that followed, it nearly destroyed me.

When I graduated from North Central, we moved to Soudan, Minnesota, to begin our ministry on the Tower Reservation. A few years later, we started a work with the Baptist General Conference at Nett Lake, Minnesota, and eventually moved there.

Then came 1957. That was a very troubled year for me, as problems of many kinds came one right after the other. The pressures became so great that I could not handle them. They eventually drove me back to drinking again. At the end of that year, I was finally wiped right out of the ministry by my alcoholism.

After losing my position as pastor, we moved back to Minneapolis and I began drinking very heavily. In the days and months that followed, many things happened that I tried desperately to avoid. Perhaps the worst was when my wife left with our four children and was threatening divorce. I did not want to lose them, but it happened.

There were many other things I tried to avoid, but they happened, too. I always felt the most humiliating thing for any person would be to wake up in a drunk tank. I did not want that experience, but I could not keep it from happening, and it happened again and again and again. I did not want to be ousted from the ministry, but I was. I did not want to wreck my health, but I did. I wanted to hang onto my driver's license and my car, but I lost both of them.

Once I was out of the ministry, I had to find other means of earning a living. I was able to get a number of different jobs, but it was very painful to lose them one by one because of my drinking. Alcohol seemed to have made me non-functional. I just was not able to handle any kind of effectual role in society. Alcoholism had programmed me into non-success. I could not keep a job. I was not able to function as a husband or a father.

I was not able to do my duty as a provider.

All this was very frustrating and hurtful. These losses caused me a great deal of suffering. I tried desperately to quit my drinking. I doubled my praying and Bible-reading time, but it made no difference. I fought against it every way I could, yet nothing seemed to help. It seemed everything was against me. I knew alcohol was destroying me, but my struggle to break free was without success. I just simply could not stop.

Thus, by the time the next thirteen years had run their course, I had been arrested more than eighty-five times in different parts of the United States. I had been divorced twice by my first wife, the second time with such finality I knew we would never get back together again. I had also lost twelve good jobs because I was not able to work consistently. Eventually, I sold everything I had until I was down to just the clothes on my back. At that point, I found myself on skid row.

By this time, I could sink no lower. I had reached a point of total deterioration. All my character qualities had been destroyed. All moral and spiritual strengths were gone. As an alcoholic, I had hit bottom, not only physically, but also emotionally, mentally, socially, and spiritually. And daily, I rubbed shoulders with others who shared my bondage and whatever booze we could manage to scrounge. Among them were doctors and lawyers, Catholic priests and Protestant preachers. We all had one thing in common: alcoholism had wrestled us to the mat for the count of three, and won. We were utterly and totally defeated. None of us wanted it to happen, but it did and now we were paying the price.

It had taken me some six years to get to this point, and in my desperation I began to look around for godly men and women to help me. But look though I did, I could find no one who understood where I was at and what I was going through. There did not seem to be anyone who had the kind of knowledge needed to help me out of my problem.

Eventually, I went to a Christian halfway house, and it was here that I was able to start somewhat of a comeback. I got a job at the post office in Minneapolis and began going to an Indian church on the north side of the city. While there, I met my present wife, Betty, who was an adult Sunday school teacher. We were married in 1968.

Not long after our wedding, I fell back into drinking. It was a very rough time for Betty. She came to know what it was like to live with an alcoholic. It finally got so bad that we were on the verge of separation and divorce. Then when things looked blackest for us, Betty discovered a business card in my pocket. It had been given to me by an Indian counselor. Desperate for help, she called the number. After talking with the counselor and explaining our situation, a plan of action was set up.

"I don't blame you for thinking of separation and divorce," the counselor said, "but before you take that step, I think you should try getting Art into treatment. I know Art. I know his capabilities, and I think if he had a chance to go through treatment for his alcoholism, he would be able to make it."

Betty was not too sure at first. For one thing, it was going to be expensive. She would need to hire a lawyer, and then there would be a daily fee based on her income to put me in treatment. This was more than she had. We were already in debt, and were about to lose our car because we were three months behind in payments. To top things off, I had just lost another job.

But the counselor continued to talk.

"The way we look at it," he said, "you have this obligation to Art as his wife. Why don't you commit him into treatment, and then if you want to leave him and divorce him, go ahead. But at least give Art that much of a break."

At last he convinced her.

"I'll give it a try," she said, "but how do I do it?"

"Come on over to my office, and we'll make plans," he said. "If you'll just cooperate with us, we'll do the rest."

After meeting with the counselor, a plan was devised and put into action that same week. With the cooperation of the court and another counselor, papers were drawn up and signed authorizing my committal. Then Betty called the treatment center to tell them that I would be brought in on a certain Saturday and that I would probably be drunk. This was the only way they figured they could get me there.

When the designated Saturday arrived, I was suffering from a bad hangover and Betty was out. After a while, she came home. For the first time in a long time, she seemed to be in quite a genial mood, but I was too sick to think much of it at the time. Before she took her coat off, she saw how sick I was and volunteered to get me something to drink.

"Get me a quart of brandy," I said.

Without a word, she went down to the liquor store and bought the brandy I craved. Then she sat there with me as I drank, and even encouraged me to drink more. This was strange behavior for her, but before I could begin to question her motives, I passed out.

Immediately, Betty was on the phone to the counselor and he took over. He and another co-worker came to our place with a policeman. Together they loaded me into a car and hauled me off to the treatment center.

When I woke up and discovered where I was, I became furious. To be in treatment was bad enough, but to be tricked into it by my wife and the counselor was unforgiveable. I vowed vengeance against them both as soon as I was back on the street.

In the meantime, I had to go through the program. It worked quite well for me, and I was released. But eleven months from the day I was first committed, I fell back into drinking. That is the way it is with a chronic illness; you can make progress for a while, but there is always the chance of a relapse.

When this happened, some of the students I had been going to school with came up to Superior, Wisconsin to get me. Once again they got me drunk so they could control me, and since my original commitment had been for one year, they were legally able to get me back into treatment. So for a second time, I woke up in the treatment center and began the process all over again.

It was this second time through that I began to sense that there was something here that could probably help. It was the working of spiritual principles which was new to me. If it could help so many others, I thought, then it would certainly be able to help me. And it did. As I began to grasp the meaning of the Alcoholics Anonymous (AA) program and its principles, I also began the long hard climb to recovery and sobriety.

Today, I am eternally grateful to Betty for the steps she took and for the courage she had in committing me to treatment. It not only sobered me up, but it saved my life. I know without a doubt, that if I had continued drinking the way I was, I would have died of acute alcoholism within a year.

But even more than this, I am thankful for the new spiritual life I have experienced. As I worked through the Twelve Steps of the AA program, I was reconciled again with God through the Lord Jesus Christ. In the years that followed, I have been able to stabilize and become the kind of Christian that I had always wanted to be, even before the problem of alcoholism reared its ugly head.

CHAPTER THREE
A Promise Fulfilled

THE ROAD TO recovery was a long one. It took me thirteen years to destroy myself, so it was only natural that the rebuilding of my life would not happen overnight. But when I left the treatment center the second time, I knew things were going to be different. At long last, I had begun to deal with my addiction on the deepest possible level, the spiritual.

Now that I was sober, I needed to find a means of livelihood. As I considered my options, I realized the thing I knew best was probably alcohol addiction. This led to enrollment in the Metropolitan Junior College in Minneapolis to study chemical dependency. Two years later, I took my first position in counseling at the Sunnybrook Treatment Center in Crookston, Minnesota. It is now called the Glenmore Foundation.

One evening during our stay in Crookston, Betty was feeling depressed. She looked at me and said, "Art, I don't even feel like I am a Christian anymore."

At that moment, I realized I was not the only one affected by my addiction. When I hit bottom as an alcoholic, I somehow dragged Betty down with me. The dawning of this understanding started us both on some deep soul-searching. Together we began to seek some kind of spiritual base upon which we could rebuild our lives.

During these years, I had been reading the Bible and praying a lot, yet it seemed to get me nowhere. Now that I realized the spiritual trouble we were in, I had a new reason for studying the Bible. I was looking for help in rebuilding our spiritual lives and, of all places, I found it in the Book of Malachi in the Bible. I was reading one day in chapter three about tithing, which means giving 10 percent of our income to God. As I read, I was really struck by God's promise. He said if we returned to God, He would return to us, and the place to begin was in giving the Lord what was rightfully His.

Betty and I discussed the matter of tithing at length, but it did not seem possible because of the way our finances were at the moment. We figured we were going into debt at about the rate of thirty dollars a month, in spite of our best efforts to manage our income carefully. Still, when we asked for God's direction, He led us to this portion of Malachi, so we decided to take Him at His word. When our next check came, we took our tithe off the top. Then, after counseling with a local pastor, we started taking out one-tenth out of our gross pay, not from what we ended up taking home. After a while, we even began to give offerings over and above our tithe. Strange as it may seem, this was our starting point in getting back on our feet as Christians.

As the weeks went by, we began to look for places where we could be fed spiritually. We asked for counseling from area pastors and started going to all the special meetings we could find. Some of the most helpful ones were the Bill Gothard Seminars. Over the years, Betty has gone four times and I have gone three. It was a direct result of these meetings that we began reading ten chapters a day from the Bible.

We also sought help from Christian books. Whenever we took a trip to the Twin Cities or Duluth, one stopping place was always the Christian bookstore. Here I bought books I thought might be helpful to me in spiritual growth, and Betty looked for the kind of books she felt she needed. When we got back home, we would read and study these books. And we prayed like we had never prayed before.

One of the biggest hurdles I had to cross in my journey back to spiritual wholeness was the matter of my dishonesty. As I began to deal with this and started making things right, it really disturbed me. One night as

I was praying, I brought this matter up to the Lord. "I thought that when we were forgiven, the past was all wiped clean," I said. "I thought this was all behind me. Now You're telling me I have to make things right."

"They are forgiven, Art," the Lord seemed to say, "but as long as those unpaid debts remain, there is still dishonesty inside you."

I realized then, that unless I cleared up these debts, I was still basically a dishonest person. The only way to solve the problem was to pay them off as I was able, and with each bill I paid, I became that much more honest. Once I came to understand this, I concentrated on clearing off these debts as the Lord brought them to my mind.

One debt I owed was to a gas station in Grand Marais, Minnesota. I went there one day to talk to the owner. "When I lost my job at the hospital, I left here without paying the bill I owed you, and I've come to pay it," I said.

"No, Art, you don't owe us any money," he said.

"Oh, yes, I do."

The owner went to his file and flipped through it. "There's nothing here, Art," he said. "You don't owe us anything."

"Why don't you check over there in that other file?" I asked.

He did and in a few moments he found it. "Sure enough, you do have a bill," he said. He brought it over and laid it in front of me.

I placed my credit card on the counter. "Put it on there," I told him.

As I was leaving, he came over to my car. We chatted for a while and then he gave me some tips on a good fishing spot. Since then, we have become real good friends.

I also had other things to make right in that town, so I took care of them, too. And now I don't have to dodge anybody in that place. A while later, I was asked to come and speak at the church in Grand Marais. As I walked out on the platform, I was suddenly very glad I had straightened things out around there. Sitting right in front of me were three of the men to whom I had owed money.

There were a lot of other areas in our lives that needed to be worked on like this. In fact, it took us from 1973 until 1986 to get back on our feet spiritually, to a point where God could use us in the ministry once again. That is thirteen years of rebuilding, the same length of time it took my alcohol addiction to bring me to the point of destruction. Today, by the grace of God, I am once again sharing the gospel with my own native people.

Over the years, I have seen my story repeated many times. In my work in the treatment centers, I have observed the struggles of many other Christians who had begun drinking, fell into alcoholism, and then had to climb the same road to recovery I did. It is no easy matter for a person to get back on his feet spiritually, for when someone hits bedrock, there is no character strength, spiritual strength, or moral strength left. Spiritual growth has to begin all over again. It is as though they are baby Christians, needing the very basic, foundational truths of the faith to rebuild their spiritual lives.

We stayed at Crookston for three years. During that time, a number of our clients were native people. Then, beginning in 1977, I worked in a half-way house in northern Minnesota for a year and a half. Since this was in the heart of an Indian reservation, I gained a lot of experience in working with Indian alcoholics. I was then asked to take the position of spiritual counselor at an all-Indian treatment center in the state. I stayed there six and one-half years.

As spiritual counselor at Mash-Ka-Wisen, I did the work of a chaplain. I listened as the clients took the Fifth Step of the AA program. This is the step where they "admitted to God, themselves and another human being the exact nature of their wrongs." I was there to listen and counsel, as they worked through a lot of unresolved grief. Though I did not keep an exact record, I probably dealt at a very personal level with close to two thousand people during those years at the center.

It was from these times of sharing that I gained a larger understanding of the struggles and inner hurts our Indian people have. After a while, with the same problems coming up again and again, we began to see a pattern. There were two things that were troubling almost every native person who came through the treatment center. These same two things, while common among the population as a whole, seemed especially troublesome to native people. One of these was the matter of unresolved grieving. The other was childhood separation from parents. The main purpose of this book is to discuss these problems that are destroying so many of our people, and then to offer concrete solutions that I know from experience can make a difference. I think it is time we stopped treating symptoms and examine the source of the problem. When we do, we will have a chance to make a major impact on the native community.

I don't claim to be an expert. I am merely sharing what I have learned through my years of experience on both sides of the alcohol problem. You may not agree with everything I say. That is your privilege. But I would ask that you keep an open mind, and that you read the entire book before you pass judgment. If you find one suggestion that will help you personally, or someone you know, then the objective of **The Grieving Indian** will be met.

CHAPTER FOUR

The Nature of Grief

READ ALMOST ANY newspaper that serves a significant Indian population, and there is close to a 100 percent chance you will find stories of tragedy. Not long ago, I remember reading three such accounts within a very short period of time. One involved four teenagers in a car-train accident which killed three of them. In the same paper, I read of a five-year-old girl who was killed by a hit-and-run driver. She was riding her bike on the bicycle path at the side of the road when a drunk driver veered off the pavement and hit her. A few days later, there was a third tragedy. A man and his wife got into an argument and he was fatally stabbed. The woman was arrested after reporting the death from a neighbor's home.

Imagine what these deaths did to the parents and other family members who still remained. No one was expecting these people to die. The four young people were out for a good time, probably on a date. Anyone who knew them would have said they had their whole adult lives ahead of them. And it was the same with the five-year-old girl. When she left her home, it was to enjoy the new skill of riding her bike. No one could have guessed that her life was to be taken so suddenly. The same holds true for the husband and wife. I am sure neither of them got up in the morning with the knowledge that one of them was going to die that day.

These deaths were unexpected. Not one of the victims had an incurable disease that was known to be devouring his life. They had not been told by the doctor that they had only a few weeks or months to live. The deaths they died were violent and unanticipated. According to Dr. Arthur Freese, a noted authority on grief, "...Sudden death causes one of the most traumatic and painful bereavements for the survivors." There is no chance for family and friends to prepare themselves for the inevitable. It just happens. One minute their loved ones are alive. The next, they are dead. Those who are left to mourn are torn apart by grief, and unless they are able to deal with it adequately, they will face some tremendous problems down the road. It is this unanticipated death that has reached more than epidemic proportions among our native people. Because of its nature, it creates a double loss. The victim is lost to the grave, while the survivors, in many cases, are lost to destructive behavior brought on by unresolved grief.

Handling Death That Is Expected

Before we can understand the violent, traumatic, unexpected kind of death, we need to see what ordinary, anticipated death is like and how it is handled. The average life span for the typical North American is around seventy-five years. Most people can expect to live that long, but not without complications. With each passing year, age begins to leave its mark on us. Certain physical limitations develop. Our joints get stiff and we tire much more easily. Many of us develop wrinkles and our hair turns gray. Men have a tendency to go bald. Though many try to cover up the signs of aging, there is not a whole lot anyone can do to keep himself young.

When family members see this happening with a parent or friend, they know that life is drawing to a close and they begin to grieve. I remember when my youngest son faced this. I was talking with him one day, and made mention of the fact that I was over sixty-five and that since I was only promised about seventy years, I probably did not have much longer to go. Well, as soon as he heard that he began to deny it right away. "Dad, you're strong and healthy, so don't talk like that," he said. "You know nothing is going to happen to you." He was in the first phase of dealing with anticipated death, which is denial. He knew in his head that death was inevitable, but he was denying it with his heart.

A similar situation can develop when a family member or a friend becomes terminally ill. Tests have been made. The doctors have examined the results and made their diagnosis. There are only a few months left to live. But how do most people react when they hear the news? They deny it. "Get a second opinion." "Somebody made a mistake in the lab." "You're looking at the wrong x-rays." "You're too good a person for this to happen to."

All of these responses are almost automatic when we first become aware of the impending death of a loved one. They are part of the first of five phases that every person goes through when grieving over an anticipated death.[2] These phases are as follows:

1. Denial
2. Anger
3. Bargaining
4. Depression
5. Acceptance.

Because the last four phases will be discussed in detail later, they are just mentioned at this time.

For most people, there is no problem handling this kind of loss. It is still painful and traumatic, but they have at least had time to prepare for the inevitable, and when it actually happens, much of their grieving is already completed.

Handling Death That Is Unexpected

Reaction to an unexpected death is quite different. Here there is no time to prepare for the loss. It comes upon family and friends totally unannounced and they must deal with it in whatever way they can. When it is not handled well and completely, problems result. This turns what is normally deep sorrow into what can be termed **pathological grief.**

Pathological Grief

Pathology refers to sickness and that is exactly what pathological grieving implies. When people who have suffered tragic, unexpected losses cannot handle their grief, or do not complete the grieving process, their emotional, mental, social and spiritual health is affected.

Dr. Edgar N. Jackson, one of the foremost authorities on grieving, says the loss of a loved one can so upset a person, he will not be able to function normally.[3] It is as though the grief over-rides the individual's usual ability to handle a crisis. When this "over-riding" is prolonged, normal grief turns pathological.

In discussing this problem Dr. Freese writes:

> When the work of mourning isn't done, when there is 'unfinished business' left hanging, when the grief work isn't carried to completion, then the bereaved person is left with many problems to surface in a variety of ways and to affect his life seriously.[4]

To give you some idea of the extent of this problem among Indian people, consider the comparison between how long natives and non-natives live and their manners of death. The average North American is expected to live 74.5 years, while the typical native person, with an expectancy of 44.5, has thirty years less.

A comparison of the manners of death is equally startling. In the dominant society, it is generally accepted that 80 percent of the population will die anticipated deaths, with only 20 percent falling victim to an unexpected, violent end. When we look at the native scene, these figures are totally reversed. Based on informal surveys and a life of involvement within my own native community, I estimate that only 20 percent of natives die anticipated deaths, while 80 percent lose their lives through such violent, unanticipated means as car crashes, murders, suicides, fires, drownings, and freezing to death.

These estimates are underscored by a conversation I had with a native community worker. We were talking about death and dying, and from her experience on a northern Minnesota reservation, she remarked, "I don't know how long it has been since we have had a death from natural causes on our reservation. Every time someone dies, it is always alcohol or drug related.''

For many native people, life is a series of grieving events, with one unanticipated death after another. When a member of the dominant society has problems facing this type of situation, there is always a health professional, a psychologist or psychiatrist who can help them work through it. But most grieving natives have no such resources, so in desperation, the vast majority try to drown their sorrows in alcohol and drugs. Then, before they know it, they have multiplied their problems instead of solving them. Not only do they have the agony of a lost loved one to deal with, but they also have a chemical dependency problem on their hands.

Unexpected, tragic deaths can also trigger a variety of other behavioral problems, including suicide. Overcome by grief, many make attempts to over-dose with any available drug. A good example of this type of change in behavior was given in a study that was done on fourteen, non-Indian, young people.[5] They all came from fairly stable homes, and each had experienced a tragic, unexpected death in their immediate families. The study found that after the unanticipated loss of a loved one, all of these young people began to develop problems. Suddenly, there was open rebellion against parents, dropping out of school, abuse of alcohol and drugs, and even sexual misconduct.

When these problems finally got out of hand, the young people were taken for counseling or therapy at one particular center. After discussions over a period of time with both the parents and their children, the beginning of the negative behavior was traced back to the time of the unexpected death of a loved one. The unanticipated death was what triggered the whole problem.

Once they saw the cause, counselors began to help each of the young people to work through his grieving.

With this taken care of, it was not long before the negative behavior disappeared. Suddenly, the drop-outs were in school again, the rebellious, negative behavior ended, and they were back to normal conduct.

Judging from the experiences of the hundreds of native people I counseled, our Indian communities may well be suffering for similar reasons. I feel strongly that if studies could be performed with Indian young people and adults who are manifesting unusual and troublesome behavior, we would probably find a lot of unsettled grief conditions. This could in measure explain the rampant delinquency, vandalism and violence so common among our people.

Other Problems Caused by Unsettled Grief

The effects of unsettled grief are not limited to the emotional and mental areas. The sudden, unexpected, violent death of a close friend or loved one can also cause physical problems. Authorities on grieving have compiled a list of as many as fifty-one such grief-related symptoms and illnesses. Among these complaints are sleeplessness, inability to work, problems with the bowels, headaches, fainting, dizziness, vomiting, sweating, convulsions, and breathing difficulties. Rheumatoid arthritis and asthma are also frequently associated with chronic grieving. Since many native people rely on drinking and medication to handle their grief, the physical problems that result from prolonged chemical abuse would make the above list even longer.

Since becoming aware of these physical reactions to grief, many examples have come to my attention. I remember one case where someone died of a heart attack. In the days that followed, members of the family and several personal friends began to develop similar symptoms. Months later, some were still showing reactions to the death. They complained of pains in the chest, difficulty in breathing, pain and numbness in the arms, and loss of appetite. In another situation, the doctor attributed an unexplainable infection to the grieving process. In a third case, two persons in grief were diagnosed as having "spastic bowel." Another was distressed by the fear of death for almost a year. One writer listed difficulty in swallowing to be a symptom. I know of a mourner who lost the ability to eat any kind of solid food for several weeks. Soup was the only thing that kept him going.

These conditions usually develop when it has been a sudden, unexpected, violent kind of death. Anyone with these symptoms should see a doctor for a thorough checkup. Some may require medication, while others just need a doctor's assurance that they are in good health. This will go a long way towards relieving them of worry and fear.

There is a caution, however, that should be observed in this area. Many people, whose only need is to complete their grief work, are put on mild tranquilizers by well-meaning doctors. This often slows down the grieving process, instead of helping to end it. Medication of this kind can also be addictive, and it is usually just as hard to get people off pills as it is to get them off alcohol. The final word on medication is up to the doctor, of course, but be sure to tell him of any unsettled grieving situations so he can make an informed decision.

Another reaction that often occurs, though not physical, is hallucinating or seeing things. Indians are much more apt to talk about this than most people. They will tell of seeing a form at the foot of the bed, or of someone looking in through the window. Some will hear the voice of the deceased speaking to them, or hear his footsteps in the room, on the stairs or in the hall. These people need to be assured that they are not going "crazy" and that such happenings are a fairly normal part of the grieving process.

While pathological grieving has a natural connection to death, it can also be triggered by other crises. Divorce, the loss of a job, the destruction of a home by fire, or the separation of children from their parents, are all causes for grieving that may get out of hand.

Many involved in the social services feel that if they could just take these "poor children" out of those poverty-stricken homes and give them a good education, proper food and decent clothing, they would amount to something. Well, they don't. Such action often creates an even bigger problem for the children. To be taken from their family, culture, and all that is familiar, then placed in a strange home, is a very traumatic experience. Many have also been sexually abused while in foster care and this makes the problem even worse. As a result, when a child comes out of this situation, he is frequently filled with an uncontrollable rage against everything that stands for authority. A number of other negative symptoms are going to arise with these children, and will be dealt with at length in later chapters.

Grief, then, is a normal emotion, but when it is not carried through to its natural conclusion, it can destroy the person. Each one who has suffered a loss, but particularly he who has violent, unanticipated deaths to face, must work through the stages of grieving. If he does not, in most cases, meaningful life comes to a stand still. Dr. Freese cautions:

> ...Only through grief and mourning can there be recovery from the loss. The person who shirks this mourning task, who represses or denies his or her grief (who 'doesn't give in') will never come out from that shadow on the floor, will never be free of the tyranny of the past...[6]

The rest of this book deals with the stages of grieving, giving particular attention to the steps where most native people have trouble. I believe the suggestions given are sound and practical. Through their application, our people have a chance to be set free from grief to pursue happy, productive lives.

CHAPTER FIVE

The Phases of Grief

IT HAS BEEN a rough day for the Andersons. Everyone is tired. With supper over, they are getting ready to relax. Walter is watching television, his wife is finishing up the dishes. Bert, their teenage son, has gone to the community center.

Suddenly the phone rings. Walter answers it. "Hello," he says. He listens for a moment, then he speaks again. "Yes, this is the Anderson's. Who are you?" There is a pause. Then Walter's face goes pale. "No, it can't be! There must be some mistake!" He is speaking loudly and he looks very upset. He listens for a few more moments, then he hangs up.

"Who was that?" Marilyn calls from the kitchen.

"The police. They think Bert was killed in a hit-and-run. They said it's him because they found his wallet. They want us to come identify the body."

"But it can't be Bert," Marilyn sobs. "He was just here twenty minutes ago. There's got to be a mistake!"

Walter and Marilyn were just told of the unexpected death of their son. And beginning with that phone call, they began their grieving process. Over the next hours, days and probably months, they will progress through ten distinct phases of grieving (listed below), but not necessarily in the exact order given. Several may happen at the same time; some may return again and again.

1. Shock	6. Anguish-Despair
2. Panic	7. Bargaining
3. Denial	8. Forgiveness
4. Numbness	9. Acceptance
5. Rage	10. Growth-Maturation

These phases of grieving are more difficult to handle than those of an expected death. Because of the violent, tragic type of loss involved, many mourners get hung up on one phase or another and cannot go on. Unless outside help is given, they will likely carry this grief with them to their graves. Those who complete their grieving, either on their own or with help, will one day learn to live and laugh again.

Let us now take a closer look at each of the phases before zeroing in on those that cause particular problems for our native people.

Shock

The first reaction of family and friends to a tragic, unexpected death is shock. The effect is much the same as a hard blow to the head or sticking one's finger in a live socket. The tragic news is causing something like this to happen mentally, emotionally and even physically. In fact, it is often wise to take people like this to a doctor. Medication may be necessary to help them through this first reaction to the loss.

Panic

After the initial shock, panic often sets in. At this stage, the person is not able to think clearly. They cannot make up their own minds or organize themselves for action. On occasion, it may be necessary to take them by the hand and guide them through this phase.

Denial

The denial phase is almost automatic. Once the news sinks in, the natural reaction is to say it is wrong. Some feel this is a form of protection. By saying "no" to the tragedy, they are able to absorb the facts more slowly, allowing themselves time to adjust. In the case of the Andersons, both Walter and Marilyn were sure there was some mistake. After all, Bert had just left the house very much alive. There was no way he could be dead. It was either a sick joke or somebody made a terrible error.

Numbness

A third phase of grief is numbness. The unexpected tragedy temporarily overloads the emotional circuits. The survivor is left somewhat dazed or numb. Often this reaction may carry them through the burial arrangements and the funeral without any display of emotion. This is probably what happened with Jackie when President Kennedy was killed. All the pictures showed her very composed. There was no sign of tears. The commentators were all saying how brave and strong she was. But this was not likely the case. She was probably going through the phase of numbness. There were probably no tears because she was unable to cry.

This numbness may also be expressed in a physical sense where parts of the body lose a measure of feeling. The length of this phase may be as brief as a few hours or as long as several days, and it is sometimes delayed in happening. In some cases, it may not appear until several months later when suddenly the hands, feet, or some other body part begins to feel numb. To be safe, this should be checked by a doctor, but most often it is grief-related and will disappear in time.

Rage

Rage is totally opposite to numbness. It burns and boils and often strikes out unreasonably. Several days may pass before it appears, but it always comes. It is at this point where many Indian people get stuck in the grieving process. Their rage comes, but it won't go away. It continues to churn inside until they either find a way to resolve it or it destroys them.

Anguish-Despair

Another phase of grieving that many native people have trouble with is the anguish and despair. This is where the pain and sense of loss hit them full force. For many, it is more than they can handle.

Bargaining

Bargaining is the phase of grief that begins to wrestle

with the acceptance of the loss, in an effort to get on with living. As the mourner works through his grief, he might say, "I could accept her death if only we had not had a fight before the accident" or "I know he can't come back, but why did he have to be drinking when he died?"

Forgiveness

Another difficult phase for those who are grieving over a tragic, unexpected death is forgiveness. During grief of this type, a lot of blame is laid in many directions. Before the mourner will be able to finish his grieving, he will need to forgive those he has been blaming for his loss. Sometimes it is the person who died. Sometimes it is God or the drunk driver. Sometimes it is himself. Whoever, or whatever, he feels is at fault must be forgiven or the grief will continue to haunt him.

Acceptance

Acceptance follows logically once a person has taken the step of forgiveness. Suddenly, at this point, a realization comes that no amount of grieving will bring back the deceased. From then on, life begins to get back to normal again.

Growth-Maturation

Once grieving starts, personal growth and development stops, and it stays that way until the grieving process is completed. This is one reason why it is so important for mourners to finish their grief work. When it is done, the person can begin to grow again and develop meaningful relationships. He will find, that while life may not be as good as it once was, it can still be very, very pleasant.

While all these phases are painful, these are the ones where native people have the most problems: rage, anguish-despair, bargaining and forgiveness. For this reason, we will look at these phases in considerable detail. The remainder of this chapter will focus on phase five, which is rage.

Rage That Destroys

Whenever I think of this tornado of emotions called rage, one client from a treatment center comes to mind. He was a big, strong male, but as he told the details of the tragic hit-and-run death of his wife, tears streamed down his face. He relived the experience in my office that afternoon—the shock, the panic, and then the anger. He spoke of buying a gun and bullets. He told how he prepared to go out and get the guy who had run her down. Fortunately for both of them, he could not find him.

He spoke of irrational thinking and of unpredictable behavior. As he sat watching television one afternoon, one of the characters was running from a crime scene. Immediately, this big Indian man pulled up the loaded gun in his lap and shot out the television screen.

He had two small children still living with him, but now the welfare agency called to say that they were going to place them in a foster home. This was the last thing he needed. His babies were all he had left, and the authorities were wanting to take them away! A violent argument followed in which he threatened to shoot anyone who came to his home. Then he sat with his gun and faced the door, but no one showed up.

Finally, in order to get some measure of relief from the anger and anguish that boiled within, he began to drink in a deliberate way. He soon realized that he was not able to care properly for his children, so he reluctantly surrendered them to the social services for placement. There still was no one to help with his grief, but at least his children were cared for. He carried all of this accumulated hurt, anger, and bitterness within him until that afternoon when he came to see me. Then, with some assistance, he began to do his grief work within my office, and later on in a group meeting.

This man came through the first four phases of grieving without any problem, but he floundered on phase five. Try as he might, he could not put this rage behind him. Had it not been for the help he got at the center, he would have been destroyed, a victim of his own grief.

Rage and Blame

In *Help for Your Grief*, Dr. Arthur Freese draws attention to the intense anger or rage that develops as people work through their grieving. He says in part:

> There is intense anger—anger with the deceased for dying, anger with the world, anger that is readily turned on the physicians or surgeons (why didn't they do their jobs better?), even anger with God (ministers are very familiar with this and how virulent it can be). This underlying anger is easily brought out and directed at anyone and anything on the slightest provocation—and can create a host of immediate and later problems.[1]

Another noted professional in the matter of grieving, Paul Tournier, a Swiss physician and counselor, has this to say about the rage that inevitably develops:

> When a man is gripped by violent passion (or rage), it stifles in him all capacity for rational thought, and even his moral conscience; he hesitates no longer, but hurls himself into action. His reason no longer serves to provide him with good reasons to justify his conduct.[2]

Rage brought on by the tragic, unexpected loss of a loved one has been around for a long time. It was so common in Bible times, that the Israelites set up six cities of refuge to protect those who had accidently caused the death of someone. They knew that man's natural reaction to this kind of loss was an uncontrollable rage that demanded revenge. Often a member of the victim's family would be chosen to settle the score. If the one who unwittingly caused the original death could make it to the place of refuge, he was protected from the avengers. The provision of these cities made it possible for true justice to be done, rather than irrational, spur-of-the-moment vengeance.

Rage and Revenge

One of the typical reactions of a person consumed by rage is to place the blame for this loss on someone or something. They feel compelled to find a place to hang their anger. Edgar N. Jackson in *The Many Faces of Grief* gives a striking example of this.

> The anger that is an expression of grief can show itself in many ways. It can be direct. A week ago, a couple of miles from where I am writing, an accident touched off a display of anger. A tractor turned over, crushing the youth who was driving it. When the physician who rushed to the scene pronounced the victim dead, the victim's brother assaulted the physician. The expression of anger was so great that the physician had to spend the next few days in the intensive care unit of a hospital.[3]

Over the years, I have heard people tell how they planned to get even with the person they blamed for their loss. I recall one man whose cousin had been killed. He was very angry. The fellow who did the killing was sentenced to prison, but the angry cousin was not satisfied. Nine months after the death, he was finally brought in for treatment. In my conversation with him, I learned that he had been attempting to do some kind of violent act so he would be thrown into prison, too. He told me, "I'm doing my best to get thrown into _____ prison because I want a chance to kill that fellow who killed my cousin."

This was the voice of anger speaking, the voice of consuming rage. It is this kind of anger that holds many of our native people in bondage. It is a driving force. It won't allow a person any kind of peace of mind or heart. It won't let a man sit down and relax. The rage keeps boiling inside until, finally, the person does something. Usually, the action is the kind the person will regret or for which he will be punished.

Rage and Religion

Anger is not always directed at another person or some object; sometimes it is directed at God and the church. A quote from Dr. Freese made mention of this earlier in the chapter, and my own counseling experience bears this out. Indian people who are going through the rage phase of their grieving will blame God at least one-third of the time, if not more, for the particular kind of death that happens. Then in the midst of this rage, they turn away from Him and the church. In essence they are saying, "I don't want anything to do with a God who would let my brother be killed like that. You say He's a God of love? Well, He could have stopped this, but He didn't, and if that is what He's like, I want nothing to do with Him."

I firmly believe this to be a major reason why so many native people have opted for other religions or no religion at all. With the percentage of unanticipated deaths so high among Indians, there is a tremendous amount of pathological grief out there that still needs to be worked through. When the church is finally equipped and ready to help our hurting brothers and sisters deal with their grief, I think we will see a revival of interest in biblical Christianity. I hope this book plays a part in hastening that day.

Rage Against Self

Another frequent target of blame during this time of rage is the mourner himself. I counseled a woman, once, who blamed herself for her father's death, which had happened nearly seven years before. Because of her sense of guilt, she had consumed a lot of alcohol over that period of time.

Her father had died from a brain hemorrhage caused by a fall down a flight of stairs in his apartment building. The father and several friends were drinking, as was their custom on weekends, when the accident happened. When she told me she was in a city two hundred miles away at the time of the accidental death, I could see she probably was taking the blame on herself without reason. As we talked, I tried to get her to see things differently. Our conversation went something like this.

"Were you mad at your father and is that why you pushed him down the stairs?" I asked.

She was shocked. "No, I didn't push him down the stairs. I was working two hundred miles away when it happened," she said.

"Who pushed him down the stairs, then?" I asked.

"We don't know, but we think it was one of his friends."

"Was this the first time your father drank alcohol?"

"No, he drank just about every weekend for as long as I can remember," she said.

"Was this the first time he drank with these friends?"

"No, that was their pattern. They drank together every weekend at our place."

"Were these friends in the habit of pushing him down the stairs every weekend?" I asked.

"No, this was the only time it ever happened."

"Well, if you didn't push him down the stairs, how have you managed to blame yourself for it?"

She thought for a moment. "Well, if I had been home, I would have kicked those people out and kept the accident from happening."

"But you weren't home."

"No, but I should have been, and I blame myself because I wasn't there."

"How long had you been living in that other city where you were working?" I asked.

"For more than a year," she said.

"Okay, then, let's add this up. Stop me if I'm wrong. Your father and his friends had been drinking together in that upstairs apartment for more than twenty years, generally on weekends. They had gotten along well enough that you did not find it necessary to be home every weekend to protect your father from them. You were living two hundred miles from home when the accident happened, in which your father either fell or was pushed down a flight of stairs. From this fall, he got a brain hemorrhage and later died. Am I right so far?"

She nodded.

"Alright, let's continue," I said. "You feel that somehow you should have known that this was going to happen on this particular weekend and that you should have gone home to be there to prevent that accident."

Again she nodded.

At this point I paused for a moment to get her full attention. "Only God Almighty possesses the kind of power to be able to know what the future holds. Do you think you do or should have that kind of supernatural power?"

She smiled. "No, it sounds crazy, doesn't it?" She said.

"What did the coroner say about the death?"

"That it was an accidental death due to brain hemorrhage."

"Then please try to believe him and the officers who investigated the accident. If you were to blame, that would have been determined in the investigation and the law would have tried you for murder. But you weren't. You weren't even there."

She nodded in agreement.

I continued. "An accident is something that no one is able to prevent. When an accident occurs, everything comes together in a split second and nobody can do anything to keep it from happening. Many times an accident isn't even anybody's fault. Your father would probably have fallen, even if you were there."

"Well, then, if I couldn't have prevented the accident, even if I was at home, I'm not really to blame for it," she said, looking me square in the eye for the first time. Then she smiled rather sadly. "I only wish someone could have helped me with this problem soon after it happened. It's been hard to carry the guilt all these years."

Once she was given help, this woman was able to recognize her own faulty, irrational thinking. The chances are great that she was then able to complete her grieving and get on with normal, productive living. This problem with irrational thinking is typical of people who are consumed by rage. In almost every case I have dealt with, there is some kind of blaming that doesn't really make sense. Without help, this false blame sticks in the person's mind, and twenty or thirty years later, he is still blaming himself, God, or that other person or object.

Rage and Faulty Thinking

Rage also affects the kinds of decisions that are made by people who are in the process of grieving. Because of the fierce anger they are experiencing, their ability to reason is impaired, and their moral judgment is no longer functioning. Yet, like Tournier says, there is a great urge to take action, any action.

The grieving person seems to be unable to take this loss sitting down. Unfortunately, the steps that are taken would almost never be considered if the individual had full use of his senses. This is when the mourner goes out to get the guy who killed his loved one or, as was mentioned, he attacks the doctor who brings the bad news.

On this matter of faulty thinking, Dr. Freese says:

> The only protection the bereaved really have here is know-ledge—the awareness that they must not fully trust their own thinking. For they think they are being entirely rational in their decisions and actions, when actually they are totally irrational. Neither judgment nor thinking can be fully trusted during any of the stages of grief. [4]

Authors Bernadine Kreis and Alice Pattie in *Up from Grief* are even more pointed in their observations. They write:

> Most grievers find that acting on those first tentative plans is dangerous, especially irreversible decisions like selling your house, moving away, or changing jobs. [5]

I once counseled an Indian woman who had lost a daughter. She had been shot by someone they knew during a drunken brawl. The mother came to my office and we talked about it.

"Art, I don't know what I am going to do with my boys," she said.

"What's the matter?" I asked. "Are they being threatened, too?"

"No," she said, "but they and some of the others all want to take up their rifles and get this fellow, and I don't know if I am going to be able to stop them from doing it."

Right away, I could see the uncontrollable rage and signs of irrational thinking. All the relatives of the victim wanted this fellow dead. There was a strong thirst for blood and vengeance. This woman and her family had quite a problem with that.

We talked further, and just before we parted, I said, "You're going to be illogical in your thinking, now, because of the anger that you feel over this. Be careful not to make any major decisions without seeking some outside advice. Don't sell your home. Don't quit your job. And don't move out of the area."

She looked startled. "Art, who's told you about us?"

Now it was my turn to be puzzled. "What do you mean?" I asked. "Nobody has told me anything."

"You hit the nail right on the head," she said. "That's exactly what we were going to do. I was planning to quit my job. We were going to sell our home, and we were going to move back to my home state."

"Do you have a place back there where you can live?" I asked.

"No."

"Do you have a job back there?"

"No, I don't."

"Well, do you have any idea how you will make a go of it once you get there?" I asked.

"No."

"Well, then, it sounds to me like you have been doing some very irrational thinking."

"My mother-in-law has told us the same thing—don't sell, don't move, and don't quit your jobs," she said.

I could see this woman was being given sound advice, so I told her to take it. "It seems to me your mother-in-law has her head on straight. For the next year, don't make any decisions without telling her your plans. Then, whatever she suggests to you, you had better listen, because she is rational, but you will not be."

To this woman, and thousands like her, the plans that are made seem perfectly logical. There is no sense of being in error because their normal thinking processes have been disrupted by grief.

Anger, then, is one of the major stumbling blocks for native people, especially those who are mourning over an unexpected, tragic death. The uncontrollable rage, the illogical thinking and the placing of blame have trapped countless thousands of our people in a prison of grief. Wise counseling can be a key to setting them free.

CHAPTER SIX

Grief and the Alcoholic

A MAN CAME into my office one day at one of the counseling centers where I worked. He wanted to talk about the death of his wife. She had been well-liked in the neighborhood and well-known. As long as she was alive, their home was busy with people coming and going. There was always someone visiting.

This man was used to the activity, so when his wife died and the funeral was over, he thought people would keep coming, but they didn't. He went back to his home and waited, but no one came to talk with him. He had no company. The hours went by, and still he was alone. Finally about ten o'clock in the evening, he couldn't take it anymore. He was filled with such anger at the coldness of the people who left him to handle his grief alone that he had to strike back. He put on his jacket, headed down to the liquor store and began his drinking. The end result was his eventual commitment to the treatment center where I worked.

This man is a good example of what happens when pathological grief is left untreated. Wise King Solomon asks several questions and then answers them very pointedly in Proverbs 23:29, 30. He says, "Who has trouble? Who has sorrow? Who is fighting? Who is complaining? Who is hurt without a reason? Who has eyes that have become red? Those who stay a long time over wine. Those who go to taste mixed wine." When I look at these verses, I see a perfect picture of a grieving person with an alcohol problem—sorrow, weeping and lingering long over wine.

The man described at the beginning of this chapter fits this picture very well. Our emotional and mental make-ups are so closely linked to our physical bodies that when one part is afflicted in some way, another part of our being may show the reaction. In the case just stated, the rage and hurt this man felt at the neglect of his neighbors resulted in a severe addiction problem for him.

The Effects of Unresolved Grief

Over the years, research into the effects of unresolved grieving has determined that one or more of five different reactions are likely to surface. The first reaction, as shown in the above illustration, is addiction to alcohol, drugs or both. Other reactions include mental illness and acute depression. Those who suffer from these often attempt suicide and a good portion of them will be successful. A fourth reaction is abuse of food to the point where the person becomes grossly over-weight. Neurotic behavior is the fifth common reaction. As I think about the clients I have seen, most of them have shown at least one of these, and some have had all five.

Among natives the most common reaction is that of alcoholism. An estimated 80 percent of our people have a major drinking problem. They may not all be alcoholics, but they at least are drinking to the point where it affects their lives and the lives of their families in a negative way. This problem is so severe, that this entire chapter is devoted to the subject.

Understanding Addiction

The years 1958 through 1970 were the "ugly years" of my life. During this time my addiction problem, which had never been dealt with, re-asserted itself, and I suffered relapse after relapse. I wanted desperately to live a good, stable, Christian life, but I just could not.

After I completed treatment for the fourth time, I heard a lecture on addiction. It informed me of the great strengths of my mortal enemy, alcoholism. Like Samson of the Bible, who was betrayed by Delilah, we must grow our seven locks of hair again before we can rise up and defeat our enemies. This lecture also taught me about the power of addiction and why it has been such a barrier to developing a strong, enduring Christian character. I knew this was not only my problem, but also the problem of vast numbers of our Indian people. It was not that we did not want to serve the Lord. We did. But in spite of our best efforts to remain sober, we found ourselves back to drinking again and again.

I learned that addiction is an uncontrollable, overpowering urge, drive, or force, that becomes stronger than all other drives. It becomes the most important thing, and the most demanding thing in our lives. There doesn't seem to be anything more powerful than those addictive needs. Addiction becomes the one primary urge that demands satisfaction above all else.

It is hard for most people to understand this. Normally, the most powerful needs we have are hunger, sex, and survival, but addiction is stronger than all of these. It is more important, more urgent, than hunger, even stronger than sexual drives. It overpowers the need to survive. Doctors told many of us what alcohol was doing to our physical systems, but we went right back to drinking in a very short time. In spite of the warning, many of our drinking buddies drank themselves to death.

The people around us who witness this behavior conclude we must be crazy or insane, or absolutely devoid of any kind of moral strength. Certainly that is what it feels like and it leads many an alcoholic to suicide, not realizing that the root of the problem is a physical addiction. They have lost the meaning and purpose of life and feel there is nothing left to live for. I know. I have been there. If these people understood their addiction, and the fact that we have a program that can effectively arrest it, how differently they might react to it all.

Addiction is very powerful and it is highly underestimated. The Apostle Paul wrote in the Bible, "For I want to do good but I do not. I do not do the good I want to do. Instead I am always doing the sinful things I do not want to do" (Romans 7:18, 19). I know this is talking about sin in general, but it also applies so well to chemical dependency. Addiction is the thing that causes us to do what we don't want to do, and renders us incapable of doing what we know is right.

The urge to satisfy an addiction is automatic. It is like instinct. It triggers itself, and comes and goes of its own accord. This urge is independent of all other urges in a person's life, inside or outside. It seems to come and go in a cycle. Things like tension, depression, and excitement can stimulate the urge, or need, to "take" something, but they are unnecessary. The urge to become intoxicated can trigger itself as our other needs and "instincts" do.

The urge to satisfy an addiction is incurable. It is a chronic state, much as diabetes and leukemia are. Once you have them, you have them for life. We talk of arresting these diseases, never of healing or curing them. Once a person is addicted, the experience of intoxication has been indelibly etched within the mind. It remains the most intensely personal experience one can undergo. As time passes, with sobriety or staying clean, the urge becomes less powerful and does not recur as often, but it does return.

Overcoming Addiction

Having said all this about the power of addiction, I must not leave you with the impression that there is no hope. There is. Some find spiritual solutions. Others need both the spiritual and treatment approaches. Take my family for example. I am one of six children and we all had major problems with alcohol and drug dependency. Of these six, two invited Christ into their lives and were delivered from their alcoholism. Both are serving the Lord today. Another brother and I have needed the help of Alcoholics Anonymous to sober up. Once that happened, we were able to re-commit our lives to Christ and are now living consistent, stable Christian lives. The last two also became Christians, but since they did not deal with their addiction problems, they suffered relapse after relapse. Both eventually died of acute alcoholism.

I accepted Christ in 1947 and graduated from Bible school without ever dealing with my alcohol addiction problem. The church, the Bible school, Christian friends and fellow ministers were not able to help, though they tried diligently for more than thirteen years. I would repent, return to church for a while, and then relapse. I continued to do this over and over again, in spite of my best efforts to change. I had to go through treatment for chemical addiction four times before I was able to understand the spiritual principles of the AA program and come to practice them. Certainly God delivered me from my alcoholism, but He used the AA program and the treatment centers to do it. I also know that if I were to take another drink, then 10,000 would not be enough.

AA and the Alcoholic

The AA program consists of twelve steps, based on some very sound spiritual principles. Step Three says, "We made a decision to turn our will and our lives over to the care of God as we understood Him." In so doing, we should be making a strong commitment of our wills to a new way of life, a way of life governed by spiritual guidelines.

In my own experience, I needed to get in touch with the truth, to embrace it, to live by a new standard of rigorous honesty and integrity. I had to make restitution to those I had harmed or cheated. I had to learn to forgive. As an AA member, I came to understand that humility must become a new characteristic of my life, and that I must commit all my shortcomings and defects of character to God, and ask Him to remove them. Then according to Step Twelve, I was to become a "missionary" to other alcoholics, since no one else was having any success in helping them to recover and maintain sobriety.

By becoming involved in these principles, I found myself able to stay sober at last. Seventeen years have now passed since I took that last drink. I did not like AA at first. I tried every other avenue that offered hope. Then, as a last resort, I turned to AA, and found the help I needed. Since then, I have often wondered why I had waited so long. I thank and praise God for the good sobriety I have attained and maintained. And I thank Him, too, for the AA program which He used to bring about my lasting sobriety.

Alcoholism and Spiritual Bankruptcy

One thing I learned from my thirty-five years of drinking is that when a person hits bottom as an alcoholic, he also hits bottom spiritually. He arrives at a place where he has no character strength, no moral strength, and no spiritual strength left. This is a pathetic place for a person to be, but it's where every alcoholic ends up, including myself.

I went through Bible school. I was trained for ministry and I even served as a missionary before I fell back into drinking. I am sure many a person who had worked with Indians thought that all old Art had to do was repent, and return to the Lord, and he would be right back up there where he was. But it doesn't work that way. It needs to be understood that when a person hits rock bottom this means spiritually, too. As I shared in my personal story earlier in the book, once I sobered up, my wife and I had to begin to rebuild our spiritual lives from scratch. There was no quick cure. It took thirteen years of growth before God finally saw that we had matured enough to be used again in ministering to others, as I had when I first got out of Bible school.

Alcoholism and the Church

I am going to say something in this section that will upset some people a great deal, but I feel strongly that Christian leaders and church people need to hear it.

From reading my Bible, and knowing what it teaches, I should think the best place for an alcoholic to live would be in the shadow of the church. It is here he should be learning to rebuild his life based on biblical principles. I firmly believe the church has the answer, and all the spiritual power necessary, to get people with addiction problems back on their feet. Every alcoholic should be able to come to the church today and get the help he needs. Unfortunately—and I know there are exceptions— alcoholics are shunned by most churches. Unable to get the help they need from the most logical source, statistics tell us that 75 percent of alcoholics die in their alcoholism.

I remember a conversation with the Rev. Gordy Grimm, head chaplain at Hazeldon Treatment Center, Center City, Minn. He told me of a survey taken in 1973 among alcoholics who were in recovery. Sixty-seven percent of them said, "We went to the church first. We went to the clergy in our desperation for help, but we didn't get it, so we had to turn to AA and there we found the help we needed." Also in that survey, 68 percent of the respondents who had major mental and emotional problems said that they too went to the church and the clergy for help, but with the same result. "We couldn't find it. We had to turn to psychology and to psychiatry for that help," they said.

As a member of the clergy, I blush with shame when I hear this kind of testimony against the church. This should not be. There is something missing, a gap that needs to be filled. From what I can see, treatment programs like Alcoholics Anonymous are almost the only alternative. The fact of the matter is, 67 percent of the alcoholics who are sober today have been sobered up through AA.

I found the strength of AA to be in the way it helped establish the individual in living by spiritual principles. In my case, one of the principles I so badly needed was honesty. The church should have been doing that for me, but it wasn't. I was never taught anything about living by spiritual principles like that, but AA forced me to do it. They made it plain. "If you don't start becoming honest with the group, with yourself, and with God, then get back out on the street until you're ready, or until the stuff kills you." Faced with that kind of alternative, I had no choice. I had to think about some real turning around. I knew if I was going to make it, I must start doing what this program was telling me to do.

Today, as I look at both the church and AA, I am forced to say that what the church has not been able, or willing, to do, AA has done. It was AA that finally got me to functioning as a Christian should. For that reason, I have a lot of respect for that program. It opened the door for me when everyone else said that there was no door.

I think the church is missing a tremendous opportunity by not making use of one of the various addiction programs and the variety of local secular treatment centers. At the same time, the church must be careful not to abandon the people it has placed there. Visitation is a must. Be there to show you care whenever visiting is allowed. And be there as the individual progresses from one step to the next. If you are concerned that he needs faith in more than a mere higher power, be there to point him to the God of the Bible revealed in the person of Jesus Christ. As the need for building on spiritual principles is taught, use your Bible to give him the biblical foundation he needs.

Alcoholism and Education

If the church has been largely ineffective in ministering to alcoholics, I feel one reason may be the lack of appropriate training in Bible colleges and seminaries. I know of many of the missionaries who have done their utmost to deal with the needs of their native congregations. They have worked with prayer and zeal and devotion to God, but without much to show for their efforts. Part of the problem was they lacked the knowledge they needed. The training we have today is not offering us much of anything that will help us deal with the specific problems that Indians face, especially in the areas of grieving and alcoholism.

Two Problems, Not One

Though I have spoken highly of the merits of AA, even programs like this are not the full solution. From my experience of working with Indians in alcohol treatment centers, I have had a growing conviction that for most Indian people alcoholism is a symptom. It indicates that another problem, usually that of pathological grief, is the cause or root of the addiction. To treat one without the other is to leave the job half done. The sober, but chronic, griever is still not going to grow spiritually, and eventually he will slip right back into drinking. If it was pathological grief that triggered the alcoholism in the first place, then we need to deal with the grief, as well as the addiction, before that person can return to wholeness.

CHAPTER SEVEN

Grief, Forgiveness and the Will

I COUNSELED WITH one man—I'll call him Pete—who lost his five-year-old daughter. She was killed in a traffic accident right outside his home. Apparently, they lived on a corner lot, and one day a drunk driver failed to make the turn. His car tore across the lawn and hit the little girl. She died right there on the grass in front of her parents. The driver was arrested and eventually sent off to prison for a lengthy term.

A while later, Pete came in for treatment, and when the staff determined he had a grieving problem, they sent him to me. As I worked with him, I was amazed at the anger he expressed. There was just no way he was going to forgive this guy. He said, "Art, in another two years, the man that killed my little girl is going to be getting out of prison, and I've got a plan. I am going to be waiting for him when he is released, and I'm going to settle the score."

This man had uncontrollable grief. His rage had built to the extent that he could kill. I looked at him a few moments before I spoke. "If you do that, Pete, you realize of course that you might be spending some time in prison for this. Your own life will be ruined, and on top of that, you're going to find somebody else is going to want to pay you back. Some family members of his, possibly children, are going to put the tag on you for what you did to their father or brother or son. You may kill him, but nothing will be resolved. If I were you, I would try to see if I could clear this matter up some other way, and get my own life back to functioning.

You have already wasted a lot of years. Don't you think it's time to put this all behind you and get on with living?"

We talked this thing through for a long time, but there was no way he was going to forgive, so we dropped the subject. The man went back to his room, and I did not see him again for several days. Then one day, he walked into my office and sat down. We talked about things in general for a little while, before he finally got down to business.

"You know, I've been thinking about my case," he said.

"You mean your daughter's death?" I asked.

"Yes," he said. "You made mention of forgiving."

"That's right. Have you been thinking about forgiving him?"

He nodded. "Art, if that guy had only been sober, I think I could forgive him, but he was drunk."

This was a good sign; Pete was beginning to bargain. "He's also in jail," I replied. "He's paying for his crime against your daughter, but you're the one who is suffering. You've refused to forgive this fellow, and look at what it's doing to you. It would seem to me that God is letting this man be your tormentor until the day you forgive him."

I could tell he was thinking about what I said, so I continued. "Do you suppose he is as upset as you are?" I asked.

He shrugged in a grudging way, but made no comment.

"I think he probably dealt with this problem, and asked God to forgive him, and one day, he will probably come and ask for your forgiveness, too. This whole accident is probably not a problem to him any more. But look at you. You're the one who is tormented. Every time you think of your daughter, or this fellow, your rage boils up inside you again. Isn't that right?"

Pete nodded. "Yes, it sure is. There is hardly a day I

don't feel that torment,'' he said.

"And you'll keep on feeling that way until the day you forgive this man,'' I told him.

Bible Examples of Forgiving

Whenever I counsel people who have problems like this, I like to turn to the Bible. There are several passages of scripture I use. One is the story in Matthew 18:21, 22 where Jesus tells the disciples to forgive "seventy times seven" times. What He was really saying is that nobody can hurt us so much that we don't have to forgive them. As far as God is concerned, forgiveness is always expected and required. Another story is that of the two debtors in Matthew 18:23-25, and I used it that day with this grieving father.

"Pete, your situation reminds me of a story in the Bible. It's about two people who owed money. The one debtor owed about ten million dollars to his master, while another man owed the first debtor ten dollars. When the day of settlement came for debtor number one, his master said, 'Well, did you bring in your money? That ten million dollars you borrowed is supposed to be paid back today.'

"The first debtor hung his head. 'No,' he said.

"And why not?' the master demanded.

"'I just don't have it yet,' he said.

"Well, an agreement is an agreement, so the master turned to the people in his office and said, 'Okay, you take this man and his wife and children and sell them in public auction as slaves. Then do the same with the farm, with the house, the crops and everything. Bring all the money in and we'll close this case.'

"When the first debtor heard this, he fell on his face before his master and pleaded for more time. 'I don't intend to rob you of a single cent,' he said. 'I'll pay back every penny, but I need more time.'

"The master listened to the pleas of the debtor and felt sorry for him. 'Okay, get up and go home,' he said.

'I'm going to forgive you for this whole debt.'

"So the first debtor got up and went out. As he was going home, he met the man who owed him ten dollars. The Bible says he grabbed him by the throat and demanded his money right there. When the man could not pay, the first debtor had him thrown into jail.

"Now there were other people on the street who saw what happened. They returned to the master and told him all about it. The master was very angry. He ordered the first debtor to be brought before him again. 'If I could find the compassion to forgive you for ten million dollars, couldn't you have enough pity to forgive your brother for a ten dollar debt?' he asked. Then he turned to his servants. 'Take this fellow to the tormentors, and leave him there until he pays every penny of that ten million dollars.'"

When I finished telling the story, I tried to make sure Pete got the point. "You're just like the first debtor," I said. "Since you are unwilling to forgive the man who killed your little girl, God has turned you over to the tormentors until you are ready to change your mind. And that's where you are going to stay until you take steps to clear this up."

This was what finally moved him to begin thinking of forgiveness, and once this business of bargaining began, I knew he was on the way to completing his grieving. From there, it would only be a short way to full recovery.

The Will and Indian People

To forgive someone who has wronged us greatly is not easy. Our heads, or our intellects, may tell us there is no reason to forgive; the person who harmed us deserves to be hated. Our hearts, or emotions, will likely give us a similar message. If forgiveness depended on these two levels of our beings, it might never happen. But every human being also has a will and this is the key to forgiveness, even in the most difficult circumstances. By exercising our wills, we can overcome impossible odds.

Unfortunately, many Indian people have an extra stroke against them when it comes to the will. Social programs, cultural influences, and the different government departments in charge of Indian affairs, have deprived large numbers of our people of the right of exercising their wills. As a result, many native people are excessively passive rather than active. By passive, I mean there is non-use of their will and intellect.

A good example of this is a native community I'll call Lake Passive. The people there are observers, not joiners. Over the years different churches have come to the community, but nobody will take an active part. No one wants to identify with one group or the other. They might attend the services and listen to whichever clergyman might be there, but no one will make a commitment to follow this faith or that one.

The same type of situation shows up with the use of the intellect. When young people attend classes in Lake Passive, it is not popular to answer questions properly. If someone knows the answer and responds accurately, he is jeered and put down for it.

This problem of being passive also spills over into the area of self-government. When the elders learned they were going to be expected to take control of their own affairs, there was a lot of panic. People were scared to death of having to make some decisions that would involve their own welfare. "What's going to happen to us? What's going to happen to our children?" were the anxieties that were expressed.

Indian people took excellent care of themselves up to about three generations ago, then problems began. That's about the same time the U.S. and Canadian governments began to take control of the lives of native people. Before then, our people were very self-sufficient. Since that time, over the last sixty years or so, they have become dependent. To my way of thinking, this problem has its roots in government control. Because native people no longer needed to make crucial decisions regarding their personal affairs, their once active wills became passive. Today, many find it almost impossible to act on their own behalf.

But this is not a problem peculiar to Indian people. The Jews faced it in the Bible, and so have the Blacks in the U.S. With the Jews, it showed up after they spent 430 years in Egypt, much of the time in bondage. The last generation or so knew nothing but slavery. Then along came Moses, who was supposed to lead these people to the promised land. Everyone was excited about it, but once they crossed the Red Sea and entered the wilderness, Moses had a big job trying to work that slave mentality out of them. In the end, most of them had to die in the wilderness because they were slaves at heart, and God needed "free" people to enter the promised land. It took a whole new generation, young people who had not been drilled in being passive, to meet this requirement.

With the Blacks in the U.S., it was much the same. Those who have studied the civil rights struggle say it took many years to get that slave mentality out of people's heads. Only when that happened were they able to start taking responsibility for their own affairs. John M. Perkins, in his book called *Let Justice Roll Down*,[1] talks about the condition of the church among Blacks during this time. He reports that there really was very little spiritual life. I assume this was largely because the people had few occasions in which to use their wills. Most of their decisions were made by their owners, leaving the majority of Blacks very passive.

The Will and Decision-Making

This matter of passive wills makes a major difference in how native people handle decision-making, especially in the spiritual realm. When there is a problem with alcohol addiction, the person must decide to go with something like the AA program, and AA is very unpopular with most drinking people. Then each of the steps within the program requires a conscious decision. For instance, Step Three asks for a decision to turn our will and our lives over to the care of God as we understand Him. When someone has been programmed to avoid decisions, this becomes a very difficult step.

In counseling people like this, I say, "You're never going to sober up until you make this decision. It won't be easy and it won't be popular, but you've got to do it or you will never break free from your alcoholism." Eventually, they either give in and make a conscious decision and are helped, or else they avoid it and die from acute alcoholism. In the latter case, it is as much their passive will that killed them as it is the alcohol.

In dealing with people who want to make a personal commitment to Jesus Christ, this matter of passive wills also comes into play. Unless a person is willing to make a conscious decision to follow the Lord, nothing much is going to come of praying the sinner's prayer. To handle this situation, I type out a prayer of repentance asking God for forgiveness and salvation. It might read something like this:

Dear God, I have done many things that are wrong in Your sight. I am a sinner and I need Your forgiveness. I believe that Jesus died in my place, that He was buried, and that He rose again on the third day to make us right with You. I believe the blood of Jesus can make me clean from all sin. Right now, I am accepting Jesus Christ as my Saviour from sin and as the Lord of my life. I pray that You will not only forgive me, but that You will also give me a new heart so that I will be able to forgive others who have harmed or hurt me. Thank you for giving me life that lasts forever, and help me know for sure that I am now a child of God. I am asking You for all of this in Jesus' name. Amen.

Then I let the person read it.

"Is there anything here you object to?" I ask.

"Well, no, not really."

"Okay then, you take this with you, and one day whenever you feel you're ready to make your decision, then you take out this paper and pray this prayer out loud. These aren't magic words. They are an agreement between you and the Lord. He needs to hear them coming from your heart and lips. Maybe you will want to go into your bedroom and shut the door, or you may want to go out for a walk where you can be alone, but you need to pray this prayer and you should do it out loud. If you do it now, you might be doing it to please me. I don't want that. It is much better if you make this decision when you are by yourself. Then it will be your decision and it will be between you and God."

As I continue talking to this person, I explain what it means to become a Christian and that it will not be easy. "If you're going to commit yourself to this, you're going to want to think it through. Are you willing to pay the price of being a Christian? It's not a popular way to go. It is much easier to follow the crowd. Becoming a Christian means you are going to pattern your life by Bible standards no matter what comes your way. When you are ready to make that kind of decision, then that is when you need to pray this prayer." Usually people will rise to this kind of challenge. And when they make a decision in this way, it becomes a lasting decision, not an emotional dead-end.

Using the Will to Forgive

Now that we have established the importance of the will in making decisions, we need to look again at forgiveness and its role in the grieving process. When it comes to forgiving, the will is what counts. A decision must be made to forgive the person or persons who have wronged us. If it isn't, we will never get over the grieving, and in the end the bitterness and anger will destroy us.

Let me give you an example. In one of my seminars, I heard the story of an Indian girl who was raped by three men. She knew who they were, but they got away with it. For some reason, the law did not punish them, and she was left to suffer the effects of this wrong. The chances are her rage will eventually destroy her unless she can come to the point of forgiving these men for the crime they committed. Her emotions will naturally tell her "no." Her intellect will hold up the law and say they broke it and therefore deserve to be punished, not forgiven. All she has left, then, is her will. In order to cut herself free from this grieving situation, she has to make a conscious decision with her will to forgive, in spite of what her emotions and intellect tell her.

Forgiving is not easy, and it is not something that happens instantly. The will to forgive must continually be reaffirmed until the intellect and emotions have been brought in line. In this girl's case, some bitterness is bound to surface for a while. The day after the decision is made to forgive, all the old injuries and feelings are going to start building up again. That is a sign she needs to continue to work on forgiveness. Her emotions and intellect must be brought under the control of her will. She needs to get tough with herself. "Okay, Mary, cut this out. I forgave those guys yesterday at ten o'clock in the morning, and that stands. I've been wronged, but I have forgiven them and now I am going to get on with my life." Forgiveness, in this fashion, is hard work, but it can be done when it is approached through the will.

The Price of Rage

The penalty for refusing to forgive is staggering. Pete, at the beginning of this chapter, ended up an alcoholic and was planning murder because he refused to forgive. A woman I know paid a different kind of price because of her rage. Her daughter had been molested by a religious man in the community, and this woman was out for revenge. A friend of mine talked to her about it, but she vowed she would never forgive that guy, and she hasn't. A year later, my friend talked to her again. She still was crusading to get justice for her daughter, and she still was filled with bitterness and rage.

That was quite a number of years ago, now, and my friend just recently saw the same woman. When he asked her how things were going, she spilled out a gut-full of venom. "I'll never forgive that man as long as I live," she hissed. She thinks she is getting revenge, but all this hate and rage is destroying her. Her family is breaking up, and her life is hell on earth. Though all she can talk about is making that man pay for what he did, she is the one who is paying.

Getting Even—You or God?

The Apostle Paul has some sound advice on this matter.

When someone does something bad to you, do not pay him back with something bad. Try to do what all men know is right and good. As much as you can, live in peace with all men. Christian brothers, never pay back someone for the bad he has done to you. Let the anger of God take care of the other person. The Holy Writings say, 'I will pay back to them what they should get, says the Lord.' If the one who hates you is hungry, feed him. If he is thirsty, give him water. If you do that, you will be making him more ashamed of himself. Do not let sin have power over you. Let good have power over sin! (Romans 12:17-21).

Basically, Paul is saying that our job is to forgive and show kindness; God's job is to do the avenging. This is contrary to human nature, but it is the only way to handle the rage and pain that comes with grief. The old Sioux method of settling the case where the girl was raped by three men was based on revenge. The relatives of the victim would single these three fellows out, either one by one or together. Then they would break their arms and legs. In this way, they figured they had righted the wrong. This is typical of revenge done on a human level.

The Sioux method is one way of dealing with criminal behaviour, but Paul is suggesting a better way. He says we need to consider God in all of this, and he gives some strong advice on how to handle such problems. He says, "Don't take revenge, but leave room for God's wrath."

When I deal with people who are filled with hot, uncontrollable anger, like this woman who was raped, or like the father whose little girl was killed, I like to point them to this scripture. I would say, "If you think you're mad about what happened, imagine how God feels about it. He's even angrier than you are. He wants to take vengeance for you, but He also has set up a justice system. If you go ahead and take revenge against those guys, then you have taken it out of God's hands and He will stay out of it. But if you really want to be avenged and be healed of the hurt that you have suffered, then turn this whole matter over to God, and ask God to avenge you. He's ready and willing to do it. You see, these men did not break a law you made, or your family made. They broke God's law, and since they broke a law God made, He says, 'It's my right to avenge.'"

I put this into practice one time when a woman came to me for counsel. She was grieving over the unexpected, tragic loss of her husband, when another man came into her life. He promised marriage as soon as he could afford it, and in the meantime convinced her to let him move in with her. Well, she thought, as long as he is going to marry me, I guess it is okay. They lived together for a few weeks, and then suddenly this man packed up without warning and moved in with a different woman. This left her with two kinds of grief to deal with and she was very angry.

"I don't know how to handle this," she told me in my office. "I think I'm going to quit my job so I won't have to be around him anymore. I don't know what else to do, that's why I came to you."

I read Romans 12 to her and explained it.

"Well, I don't have any other way to go, so I'll try it," she said. So right there in my office, she turned to God and said, "Alright, God, I'll forgive this man if you will undertake to avenge me for what he has done to me." Then she got up and left.

Two days later she came into my office again and said, "Man, I didn't think God worked so fast."

"What do you mean?" I asked.

"Well, about him," she said. "He came into the office yesterday morning to pick up his mail. There were several letters, and he started to tear them open as he was going out the door. Then I heard him say, 'Oh, my God, no.' 'What's the matter' I asked. He turned around and came back in. 'I just got a letter from IRS. I owe them $1,800 and I have to pay it in ten days or I'm in trouble.' Then he walked out. And I said, 'God avenged me.'"

Another two days went by, and then she was back again.

"Man, isn't it marvelous how God works?" she said.

"What do you mean?" I asked.

"Didn't you hear what happened to him last night?" I shook my head.

"Well, early this morning, there was a fire in the building where he lives, and it gutted out only one apartment—his. He lost everything he owned except his car and his stereo," she said. Then she asked, "How far does God take this?"

"Well," I said, "he's still got his stereo and his car, and then his life."

She looked startled. "Oh, I don't want it to go that far!"

"Well, when you feel you have been avenged, you tell God to stop, and He will."

"I think he's had enough," she said. Then she prayed, "God, I'm satisfied. Thank you for avenging me."

That was the last time I counselled this woman. God had taken care of her problem and the rage was gone. We must be careful, however, not to make this woman's experience a pattern for handling similar problems. God is supreme. Human beings cannot manipulate Him into serving their own selfish ends. Whether or not He intervened directly on behalf of this woman, I cannot say. The important thing for her was that she committed the matter to God, and when these unfortunate things happened to the man who had wronged her, she saw God's hand in it and felt avenged. God does not promise to zap people who cross us the wrong way, but we can count on Him to avenge us. When, and how He does it, is for Him to decide, not us.

New Hearts, New Wills

We've talked about making the emotions and the intellect submit to the will, but this is only a partial solution. Our people need more than just reactivated wills. They need a whole new heart, for it is here that the emotions, intellect and will are based. And God has promised this to those who ask. In Ezekiel 36:25, He says, "I will give you a new heart." I think this is the key for not only our people, but also the Blacks and indeed the whole world. God has made a promise and we need to hold Him to it.

The Old Testament part of the Bible tells the story of God's first binding agreement with man. It is a story full of failures as man struggled to measure up to God's standard of what is right and just. Of course, there was the system of sacrifices that God demanded to make up for man's shortcomings, but it mainly served to emphasize man's basic inability to obey spiritual commands with human strength. When the Old Testament Law was first given, God said very clearly that "if you will obey me **then** I will be your God and you will be my people."

The New Testament part of the Bible brings a new element into the picture. When God saw man's lack of success in living up to divine standards, He knew something else had to be done. His remedy was to make a new binding agreement with mankind. He was speaking about this, when he wrote, "I will put my spirit in you and move you to follow my decrees and be careful to keep my laws. You will live in the land I gave your forefathers; you will be my people, and I will be your God" (Ezekiel 36:27, 28). He doesn't put in there "if you obey," because He made spiritual provision for obedience. By placing His Spirit within those who invite God's presence in their lives, He was making it so the Spirit of God within people would be drawn naturally towards the right and just standards of God. Obedience, then, would come from within and not because of outside requirements.

This new binding agreement is what I feel to be the best solution to the problem of passive, inactive wills among our people. When God gives us a new heart, we have a new base upon which to build our lives. As the need arises to forgive someone who has harmed us greatly and against whom we have great anger, we now have more than just our human strength to draw upon. All the strength of God Himself becomes available to us, as we face the object of our anger. With His help, we can say with total sincerity, and an immense sense of relief, "I forgive you."

For those who are actively involved in a spiritual ministry to native people, I feel this new binding agreement, or New Covenant, is something we need to pray about. God has made the offer and it is up to us to claim it. If we were to voice this problem that our people are in, and claim His promise to give us a new heart and to place His spirit within us, I think He would answer our prayers. Our Indian people desperately need new hearts, especially wills that are reactivated by the Holy Spirit. The Lord promises, "I will give you a new heart and put a new spirit in you; I will remove from you your heart of stone and give you a heart of flesh" (Ezekiel 36:26). In other words, He could remove a passive heart out of an individual and give him a heart reactivated by the Holy Spirit. God has made this pledge, and we need to claim it. We need to hold Him to His Word.

CHAPTER EIGHT

Breaking Loose From Grief

ESTHER'S* GRIEF HAD developed into a drinking problem and she was sent for treatment. A while later, she came to my office. I could tell she was troubled when she walked in. I offered her a chair and she sat down. I knew she had a grieving problem, so we talked for a while about the loss of her daughter. Before long, I discovered she had not done her grief work, particularly in the area of crying. "That's the trouble," I said. "You're holding back the tears and it's causing you all these problems. Things aren't going to get any better until you let yourself cry for your daughter."

For a few moments, she just looked at me. Then she shoved the books back from the edge of my desk, put her head on her arms and began to sob. In a few minutes, she sat up still crying. Then she put her head back down and cried some more. This went on for over half an hour. When it seemed as though she might be calming down, I tried to carry on with our conversation. "You really must have loved that girl," I said. This started the tears all over again. Finally, I decided to let her cry herself out.

At last, she sat up, dried her eyes and blew her nose. She looked quite composed and was able to tell me all about the death with lots of detail. Then she stood to her feet and prepared to leave. "I'm glad I came in to see you," she said. "I feel so much better, so much lighter."

She really didn't need to tell me that; I could see the change written all over her face. Her biggest need was to

* Not her real name

release her emotions, and when she did, the healing began.

The wise King Solomon once said there is a special time for everything under heaven (Ecclesiastes 3:1-8). He included in his list a time to cry, a time to have sorrow, and a time to speak. There must also come a time for cutting ties with the lost loved one, and a time to get on with living. This chapter will look at each of these as ways of bringing grieving to an end.

A Time to Listen

One of the best ways to help someone deal with his grief is to listen. This is particularly true for native people. Most are loaded down with chronic grieving, but have learned in early childhood to hold back their emotions. A sympathetic listener can help them open up to release the destructive pressure of unexpressed grief. The importance of listening cannot be over stressed. Listen! Listen! Listen! You don't have to have any particular wisdom, but you need good ears, and lots of time. The grieving person has to know that you are there for no other purpose than listening.

When I was counseling, I made sure my clients had my full attention. If I was typing when they came in, I would shut my typewriter off and push it to the side. Then I would clear everything off my desk, and turn towards my visitor. I focused all my attention on him. I listened to every word. If I missed something, I stopped him and asked him to repeat it. That way he knew I was really hearing what he said. This encouraged him to share struggles and concerns he was going through. When I say we should listen, this is the kind of listening I mean.

Sometimes it is necessary to build a trust relationship before sharing can begin. Often, what needs to be said is very personal. Someone cannot share freely if he is suspicious of you or of what you might do with what he tells you. I recall one man who walked into my office and looked around. The first thing he said was "You've got a tape recorder, haven't you?''

"Yes."

"Is it on?''

"No, it isn't." To prove it, I opened my recorder. Then I took the tape out and put it in my desk drawer. I left the recorder open so he could see it was not running.

Even this was not enough. The man kept looking around. "Is this place bugged?'' he asked.

"No."

"Well, is the stuff I'm going to tell you going to go beyond these walls?''

"No, it won't,'' I assured him.

This seemed to satisfy him, and for the first time, he sat down and began to relax. "Good,'' he said, "because I've got some real rough stuff I need to talk about.''

From this point on, he spoke freely and we were able to make good progress.

Listening is not just for professionals. Anyone who has concern for friends and neighbors can serve in this needed role. And it doesn't have to be in an office, either. Many times, as in the case of a sudden tragic death, you will find yourself in a home or at the hospital. In situations like this, it is common to hear nothing but a string of profanity, with much of it aimed at you. The best response is to sit quietly and take it. You are not really the reason for the swearing; it is merely the bitterness and hurt pouring out. Go back again in a day or two, and you may hear the same thing. Once more you need to sit there and take it. Allow them the freedom to get their worst feelings out.

This could carry on for three weeks or so before the mourner starts looking at you a little differently. If you are patient and faithful, one day he is going to start thinking, "Man, this guy took all that stuff I dumped on him without saying a word. He really must care.'' That is when he is going to start talking to you, as he probably would not be able to talk to anyone else.

Grieving people, and in particular, grieving native people, need someone to listen.

A Time to Cry

Esther's story at the beginning of this chapter showed the importance of releasing bottled-up emotions through crying. Unfortunately, this is foreign to many Indian people today. I am not sure why this hiding of emotion started, but it probably had to do with tribal and personal safety. I know at one time with my own Ojibwe tribe there was a no-crying ban. It was likely put on during the Indian wars. When Ojibwe scouts brought word that a Sioux war party was coming close, the elders warned the young people of the dangers. "We are going to be fighting the Sioux, and some of us are going to be killed," they said. "The enemy may even come into our camp. If that happens, you children run off and hide, and you hide good. And if you see some of us being killed, even if it is your mother or your father, don't you dare move and don't you dare cry."

This is when I think the no-crying ban was first put on, and I'm sure something similar happened with most tribes. It was necessary back then, but today our people need to know that the Indian wars are over. We are not fighting anybody now. Our tribal safety no longer depends on stifled cries. In fact, the bottling-up of our grief is causing more destruction today than all the Indian wars of the past put together. The only way to bring it to an end is to release ourselves from this ban so we can cry once again.

The crying ban is also practiced by a growing number of native people for religious reasons. Those who have lost loved ones are told to grieve for only four days—this number varies from tribe to tribe—and then stop. This supposedly gives the deceased person time to reach the land to which he is going. They believe if they grieve longer, it may disturb their loved one's afterlife or perhaps bring harm to the living.

This bottling up of emotion is bound to cause problems. I know of one family where some of the children followed this four-day system, while the rest of the family grieved in a normal fashion. The results were very different. Everyone in the family felt the pain, but those who stopped their grieving showed some very negative reactions—rebellion against parents, dropping out of school, and excessive drinking. Those family members who let their grief take its natural course emerged from their grieving with little or no ill effects.

Most of us in North America could learn a profitable lesson from the Jews in terms of grieving. In Jerusalem, they have a wailing wall where people can express their grief. When there is a war or some other tragedy where large numbers are lost, you will find the survivors lined up at this wall. They will pound the stones with their fists, sobbing their hearts out. This might be noisy, but it is also easing their pain.

Here, we frown on anything like that. If someone in Canada or the U.S. carried on in that fashion, well-meaning people would stop them. "Don't do that!" I've heard people say. "You'll go crazy if you don't get hold of yourself." Yet physical expressions of grief are the best things that could possibly happen. This goes for both men and women, but it doesn't mean men should cry as readily as do women, or that women should react as men do. Both, however, need to vent their sorrow, and when they do they will get through their grieving much faster.

A good example of the different ways people treat grieving happened when the mother of a close friend died. At the funeral home, people came to view the body, and then they would stop to talk and shake hands with the family. My friend found this pretty hard to handle and always started to cry. When this happened, I offered her my shoulder and encouraged her to carry on with her grieving. "It's okay," I told her. "Go ahead and cry it out." But no sooner did she start to cry, than a close relative came with conflicting advice. "Come on

now, get ahold of yourself," he said. "Knock this off."
As soon as he walked away, I told her, "If you feel like
crying, go ahead." This happened several times. One of
us was encouraging her to grieve, the other was telling
her to keep it inside.

At a workshop on grieving, I learned that there are
physical as well as emotional benefits to crying. Research shows that tears have certain properties about
them that will kill most bacteria. When the person who
is grieving chokes back the urge to cry, he opens himself up to illnesses, particularly in the areas of the throat
and lungs. That lump in the throat means there is a need
to cry. At funerals, as in my friend's case, mourners
are urged to hold in their tears. This means swallowing
the lump in their throat and bottling up their emotions.
Only harm can come from this because it is going
against nature. Crying is normal and healthful and will
be encouraged by the wise counselor.

A Time to Talk

Some of the old Indian people say we have two ways
of crying. One is through shedding tears. The other is
through talking. Both are a natural part of the grieving
process and need to be encouraged. While tears show
the pain and suffering through which the person is
going, talking allows some of that hurt to flow out into
the open. It gives the mourner a chance to put into
words the loss he feels. In so doing, the healing process
is quickened.

To my way of thinking, this therapy of talking was
specially designed by our Creator. It is so simple that
everyone can do it. By merely voicing our pain, we can
talk the hurt away. The Bible says, "Confess your faults
one to another, and pray for one another that you may
be healed" (James 5:16). While this is talking about sin,
the principle also applies to grieving. The verbal crying
of a mourner is a type of confession. Through talking it
is possible to empty out the pain, the hurt, the irrational
thinking, the rage and all the other emotions that spring

up because of grief. This is not a one-time action, but needs to be done time and again until the pain is finally gone. Once it is out of our system, we are then in a position to work through our grief and get back to normal living.

A Time for Spiritual Growth

Times of mourning are very difficult for everyone. Depression, pain and anger often leave people at the point of total despair. There is, however, something good that can come out of all this hurt. Many, when softened by the loss, make major spiritual commitments that last a lifetime.

I always find the Bible to be a big help when dealing with someone at this stage of mourning. One of my favorite parts is Psalm 84:4-7:

How happy are those who live in Your house! They are always giving thanks to You. How happy is the man whose strength is in You and in whose heart are the roads to Zion! As they pass through the dry valley of Baca, they make it a place of good water. The early rain fills the pools with good also. They go from strength to strength. Every one of them stands before God in Zion.

The valley of Baca has never been found anywhere in the Middle East, but there are different theories about what and where it is. Some Jewish scholars feel it is probably one of the hot, dry approaches to the city of Jerusalem, which sits on a hill. The temperature in those low spots is often over 100 degrees Fahrenheit. This makes it a very difficult place to travel either by foot or donkey. Yet three times a year, Jewish men had to worship in Jerusalem. Based on this, these scholars feel "Baca" talks about the hot dryness of those valleys. The travellers had to pass through them just before they climbed the hill and presented themselves to God.

A number of other writers feel there is a deeper meaning than this. To them, the valley of Baca is more a figure of speech than an actual place. They compare it to the valley of weeping, the valley of tragedy and loss, the valley of the shadow of death, the valley of mourning, grief and bereavement, the valley of pain and hurt, the valley of heartbreak, the valley of spiritual wounding. In other words, to these writers, the valley of Baca represents all the hurt and pain human beings face.

All people have some experience with pain and death. On the average, every twenty years most people will experience the death of a family member. And there are other kinds of losses that also bring great pain—the loss of a homeland, the loss of a home, the loss of family through separation and divorce. Each of these is a "valley of Baca" for that person.

No one volunteers to go through the valley of Baca. We just suddenly find ourselves in it one day. The last time it happened to me, I simply picked up the phone and there it was.

"Art, is this you?" a voice said.

"Yes."

"This is your brother, Russ." He paused for a moment. "Well, it happened," he said.

"What happened?" I asked.

"Our brother George died at twenty minutes after three this morning." Then he gave me some of the details. "Are you going to the wake and the funeral?" he asked.

I said yes, and we made plans to travel together.

"Okay, goodbye, then," Russ said, and hung up.

At that moment, I was in the valley of Baca. I didn't ask to go into it. I was just there, and I experienced that anger and all the other emotions I have been talking about. This is the way it is with so many of our native people—one Valley-of-Baca experience after another.

Another part of the Bible that goes hand-in-hand with these verses about the valley of Baca is Isaiah 61:1-3:

The Spirit of the Lord God is on me, because the Lord has chosen me to bring good news to poor people. He has sent me to heal those with a sad heart. He has sent me to tell those who are being held and those in prison that they can go free. He has sent me to tell about the year of the Lord's favor, and the day our God will bring punishment. He has sent me to comfort all who are filled with sorrow. To those who have sorrow in Zion I will give them a crown of beauty instead of ashes. I will give them the oil of joy instead of sorrow, and a spirit of praise instead of a spirit of no hope. Then they will be called oaks that are right with God, planted by the Lord, that He may be honored.

When it comes to grieving, there are two phrases in these portions of scripture that I want to emphasize. One is "oaks that are right with God," or as one version puts it, "oaks of righteousness." These are found in Isaiah 61. The other is "from strength to strength" as found in Psalm 84. God made a wonderful promise to despairing, grieving people in these verses from Isaiah. When I see the hurts of my Indian brothers and sisters, I like to claim these promises for them. No race of people is more brokenhearted and grief-ridden than the Indian race. Yet the Lord is promising to exchange this brokenness for comfort, gladness and praise. Out of the dry, barren deserts of their Valleys of Baca, He will cause oaks of righteousness to grow.

That's good news, comforting news, and our people need to hear it. Who better to tell them than those who represent the church either as clergy or laymen. I firmly believe the Christian church has the answers for our people, if we can only find enough men and women of faith to share the message. Hurting Indians need to know that the Lord can bring good out of their despair if they only will give Him a chance.

Giant oaks do not develop over night. It takes years

of slow, steady growth to produce a full-grown tree. This is where going "from strength to strength" comes in, as David wrote in Psalm 84. In the chapter on grieving and alcoholism, I mentioned how the alcoholic hits bottom in every way. He has no moral strength, character strength, or spiritual strength left to carry himself along. He is in what the Bible calls the "dry valley of Baca." It is at this point where he needs to tap into the strength that God offers in order to develop a personal strength in some area of his own life. The same is true in matters of grief. If this is done each time a grieving situation comes along, mourners will soon become the oaks God promised.

One of the first strengths that need to be developed is the ability to forgive. It is a key to completing the grieving process. In my case, I also needed to develop the strength of honesty. It was hard, but I worked at it until I paid back every debt I owed. Some may need to learn how to express love. Others may need to learn to listen to what family members are saying. The list could go on and on. As these weaknesses come to light and are presented to the grieving person, it offers a glimmer of hope, something for which to strive. He will begin to think, "These are pretty nice promises God is making. If I follow through on this (be it forgiveness, honesty or whatever), things are going to be better. Maybe it's worth it after all." And he will begin to work these spiritual principles and find himself released from the burden of his grief.

I realize many different types of people will read this book, but I need to speak directly to Christian clergy and church members for a few moments. The final words of Psalm 84:7 speak of people who have just gone through Baca and are standing before God in Zion. This says to me that the darkest moments in our lives are meant to result in spiritual progress and victory. When a grieving person is in the Valley of Baca, he probably is more open to spiritual influence than at any other time in his life. If the situation is handled properly, many will want to make a personal commitment to Jesus Christ as Lord and Saviour.

Dealing with those who grieve, particularly those who have suffered a violent, tragic loss, is not easy, but it is something everyone committed to ministry among Indian people must be ready to do. These are golden opportunities to lead people into a right relationship with God. Don't feel that a few hours of visiting at the wake and funeral are all that is needed. Grieving from normal deaths takes up to a year to complete, and when tragic, unexpected deaths are involved, it may take as long as two years of faithful counsel and help. Those who take the time to care will reap the benefits.

As Christian people, we need to help not only with their grieving, but also with their alcoholism, drug addiction, and other problems. We might have to use a treatment center, but if we do, we should be certain to maintain contact. Continuing input can be had by teaching them strength by strength what they need. Hurting people need to live in the shadow of the church. In spite of what the congregation may say about a person who has been drinking or is on drugs, give them the help they need. Invite them in and become a real brother to them even when no one else has compassion. Be different. Take them under your wing. Teach them. They need many strengths socially, spiritually, and morally. Provide that for them as this may be the only opportunity for them to go from strength to strength while in the valley of Baca. The other path for them is the route of alcoholism and drugs.

A Time to Accept Death

Just as King Solomon said, there is a time to die. The grieving person must come to understand this and be able to accept the death of his loved one. Until this happens, he cannot bring his grieving to an end. Psalm 139 is a scripture I have used many times in helping people come to this understanding. Verses thirteen through sixteen are especially helpful.

For You made the parts inside me. You put me together inside my mother. I will give thanks to You, for the greatness of the way I was made brings fear. Your works are great and my soul knows it very well. My bones were not hidden from You when I was made in secret and put together with care in the deep part of the earth. Your eyes saw me before I was put together. And all the days of my life were written in Your book before any of them came to be.

With this Psalm as a backup, I talk to the grieving person about God's wonderful plan for life, and how the lost loved one fitted into this plan. The following is an account of what our conversation might be like if I was talking to a son whose father has just died in a sudden, tragic accident. It is easier if I tell it as though it actually happened.

"I know you are feeling a lot of pain and grief right now because of your father's death, but did you ever stop to think that God is grieving for him, too?"

"He ought to grieve. He could have stopped the whole thing from happening, if He wanted to."

"It sounds like you are pretty mad at God, and that's okay. God can handle your anger, but you can't, if you keep it bottled up inside. He wants you to tell Him exactly how you feel—the pain, the anger and the sense of loss. But when you're finished, you need to listen to what He has to say. He's got answers for your questions, and He's got comfort for your heart."

"The first answer He can give me is why He killed my dad!"

"That's really not the picture as I see it, Bill. God did not kill your dad. He knew it was going to happen way back before the world was even made, but He didn't make it happen. God is not the cause of pain and suffering. He is a God of love and compassion. Right now, His heart is grieving over your father's death, just like yours is."

"But if He's God, why did He let it happen? That doesn't sound like a God of love to me."

"I think you hit the nail on the head when you said, 'let it happen.' That's exactly the way it was. God loved us so much, He refused to make robots out of us. He wanted us to be thinking, feeling human beings, so He gave us a will, and the ability to choose between right and wrong. When Adam chose to rebel, sin was passed down to all of us and we have been suffering from it ever since. Death is the penalty for that sin, and that's something even God can't change. He doesn't want it to happen. It hurts Him a great deal when someone dies, especially in an accident like your father's, but because man has chosen to break God's law, death is something we all must face."

About this time, the mourner is usually thinking pretty hard. If he is open to it, I might read Psalm 139: 13-16 to him, then I would explain what it means in relationship to his father.

"This shows you how much God cares about each one of us, including your dad. He caused him to be formed in your grandmother's womb. Then He gave life to your dad, and through him, He gave life to you. Those nineteen years you had with your father were a gift from God. I think that was very special for God to do. What do you think?"

"Yeah, I guess it was."

"You've got some good memories of your dad, I'm sure. Do you suppose at this point that you can begin to think about thanking God for giving you your dad, instead of blaming Him for his death?"

"I never really stopped to think about that. I guess I never tried to see God's side before."

At this point, a healing often begins to take place.

In cases like this where there has been some real rage against God, I will now encourage the griever to drop the charges and ask for forgiveness. I might say something like this: "You've been saying some pretty harsh

things about God because of your father's death. Don't
you think you had better tell God you're sorry and ask
for forgiveness?'' Most people will usually agree.

This psalm is a powerful tool in dealing with grief. It
has a remarkable way of starting the healing process,
and getting people ready to reconcile themselves to
God. A number of people have made a personal commitment to the Lord as a result of teaching from this
psalm.

A Time to Say Good-Bye

One of the final steps in bringing grieving to an end is
to say good-bye to the departed loved one. Here is a
typical situation. A woman has died. She is in the grave,
but the husband is still bouncing between his anguish
and rage months and even years later. There are very
painful emotions here. He cannot finish his grieving until he says good-bye to his wife.

A problem like this creates difficulties all around.
Because of his unsettled grieving, the man is not able to
show the kind of love and concern he should for his
small children and any other relatives who depend on
him. He might take care of the basics, but he is unable
to have a warm, caring relationship of any sort. Such a
man will never be able to remarry. The ties are just too
strong with his dead partner. Life has basically come to
a stand still for him because of unfinished grieving. His
only escape is to cut the emotional bond that has tied
him to his wife, and get on with living.

I counselled with an elderly man one time who had
this problem. He was about seventy years old when I
saw him, but his wife had died six years earlier. He was
so broken up he began to drink and eventually he ended
up in treatment.

One day, in one of our conversations, he told me
about a dream he had. "It was very troubling," he said.
"In the dream I met my wife. She was alive, and it was
down by our old home. We decided to go for a walk
along a trail that led into the woods. As we walked

along, I was holding her hand and we were talking about many things. Then we came to an opening in the woods, and there she stopped. She jerked her hand away and said, 'I have to leave you now.' I hung onto her with both hands and begged her not to go. It was very painful, and then I woke up. What do you think it all means?''

When someone tells me about a dream, I always pay attention to the content. Generally speaking, if the dream is of a disturbing, frightful nature, it may show that the person is still very anxious over the loss. As he progresses in his grief work, the dream content usually becomes less and less frightening. In this case, I could see there was still a lot of pain, but I wanted to hear what meaning he gave to it.

"What do you think it means?" I asked.

"After listening to your lecture, I think it probably means I have not let go of her yet," he said.

"You understand quite well," I told him. Then we talked about how he was tied to his wife and how this was affecting him. "There is one thing that might help you with this," I said. "When you get back to your room, sit down and write a letter to your wife. Put down on paper how you feel about her. Explain about your grieving and how it is affecting you. Then tell her in your letter that you are going to have to say good-bye, so you can get back to living. When you are finished, take that letter in and read it to your counselor."

Some time later, just before he left the center, he came to see me again. Treatment had been quite successful and he was all smiles.

"You look happy about going home tomorrow," I said.

"Well, I am," he said, "but last night I had another dream and I wanted to tell you about it before I went."

"Let's hear it."

"Well, it was about my wife again, and it was very much like the first dream. She was alive, and I met her at the same spot as in the other dream. We went for a walk down that path, and we talked and were having a good time. 'I'm going to have to leave you here,' she said, jerking her hand away. I nodded my head and let her go. 'I understand,' I said."

He looked at me for a moment and then he asked, "What do you think it means?"

I turned the question back to him.

"If I understand it correctly, I think it means I have been able to take back my emotions and say good-bye."

"I think you're right," I said.

If you are bothered by a problem like this, or you know someone who is, it is important to take some action. Writing a letter is one good way. If the dead loved one is buried on the reservation, it would be helpful to take the letter to the grave and read it out loud. The result of such action is almost visible as the person moves toward closing his grieving.

Saying good-bye to a loved one is not forgetting the person who has died. It is only bringing us to the end of our grieivng where the pain is gone. As long as the pain remains, the person is going to drink, or use drugs, or seek some other way of handling it.

There are also cultural ways of bringing grief to an end. In the Crow tribe, when a man dies, there are strict traditions about mourning and funerals and how the family and wife should act. The mother-in-law is the one who decides when mourning will end. At the time she chooses, close relatives will take the widow's black clothing and give her a whole new set of garments. This shows that mourning is over and it is now time for the widow to start living again. Cultural customs like this are very helpful in saying good-bye to departed loved ones, which might otherwise continue to burden the survivor.

These, then, are some of the ways people find helpful in breaking loose from grief. It is also helpful for them to realize that as tragic as their loss might be, happiness has not been destroyed forever. Things will never be the same as they once were for them, but when their mourning is over, life can still be very, very good.

CHAPTER NINE

Grief and the Separated Child

I GOT A call not long ago from a non-Indian clergyman. He had a problem. Earlier in his ministry, he and his wife adopted a native child. Everything was fine for several years, and then the boy became a teenager. Suddenly, everything blew up! A once normal child became a rebellious, violent stranger. Drugs, alcohol, skipping school, total disobedience and disrespect drove the parents to despair. The youth's entire life was out of control. They wanted to know if I, as an Indian counselor, could be of any help. I did my best, but as of yet, I do not know the outcome.

This boy is the victim of a practice common throughout Indian country—the separation of native children from their families. Some are placed in non-Indian foster homes. Others are adopted by non-Indian families. Whole generations have gone through years of separation while attending residential schools. In my own case, I spent six years there. During this long, lonely time, from when I first started school until I was a teenager, I saw my parents for just one brief summer. The situations vary, but the results are the same; the child feels abandoned and boils with rage. When he can no longer contain it, he strikes out in protest at everything around him.

Some may question my reasons for dealing with this in a book about grieving, but I feel it fits right in. Grieving is not merely the reaction to death. It is a natural expression to any major disturbance in a life. What could be more disturbing for a child than being yanked from the security of his parents' home and placed in the care of strangers? In the mind of a frightened youngster, separation by social agencies and separation by death are not all that different.

The next two chapters examine this problem in detail. My initial introduction to this problem area came through lectures and books by clinical psychologists and other experts in the field, among them Dr. Robert Hoffman. I had the privilege of listening to Dr. Hoffman on a number of occasions, as well as sharing in several workshops with him.

To give you some idea of the extent of this problem let me give you an example. Back in the 1970s, I attended a seminar conducted by Dr. Joseph Westermeyer of the University of Minnesota. He discussed the impact of separation on the Minnesota Chippewa Tribe. Altogether in the state there were about 15,000 enrolled Indians at that time. Roughly half this number, about 7,500, were eighteen years old or younger. For many years, at any one time, some 3,200 native children were separated from their homes either for foster care, adoption or schooling. That's almost half the children of the tribe!

According to Westermeyer, this number stayed the same year after year. As 200 children passed their eighteenth birthday, another 200 youngsters were being separated. By the time the second generation came along, the natural result of this process was that half the Minnesota Chippewa Tribe either had been or were presently separated from their natural families. Since then, laws have been put in place to correct this problem, but estimates say that it may take twenty-five years or longer before the results of this action are known.

The Minnesota situation is typical of other states and provinces. Across North America, separation has become almost a way of life for a large percentage of the native population. Indian leaders are aware of this problem and are taking steps to correct it. Many reservations are banding together to take on the responsibility of child and family services. Considerable pressure is being applied to bring back separated children to their natural families. Manitoba now has a law banning placement of native children outside the province. These are positive steps, but it will be many years before separation and the problems it causes have passed from the Indian scene.

Separation happens for many reasons. A medical problem such as tuberculosis can place a mother in the sanitarium for a year or two and require placement of children in temporary care. Children born to unwed mothers, who cannot or will not care for them, need adoptive or foster homes. Abuse from alcoholic parents is another common reason for separating children. Placing children in residential schools for years at a time has also been a common practice. Or it may be simply the loss of one parent through divorce, separation or death. To the child, the reason is not so important. They only know that they miss their parents and they want to go home. To make it easier to discuss, I will refer most often to foster care, but most of what I am sharing is true for these other types of separation, as well.

The time when separation takes place has a lot to do with how the child is affected. If he is younger than six months, he will usually bond, or make an attachment, to his new parents. After six months, most often he will not. In one of my workshops, we were discussing this topic, and a woman spoke up.

"We have an adopted boy and we don't have any problems with him," she said.

"When did you get him?" I asked.

"When he was two months old."

"That's what makes the difference," I told her. "He has bonded to you and your husband, just as though he was your natural child. The chances are good that you will have no problems with him whatsoever. Had he been older when you got him, the situation could be quite different.''

Separation after the age of six months leaves deep emotional and mental scars on the child. As he grows older, he begins to think a great deal about what has happened to him. He wonders why he was taken from his birth parents. The usual conclusion is that "my parents didn't care for me and so they threw me away.''

Once he decides he was abandoned, resentment and anger will begin to build inside. He will direct it towards everyone he feels is responsible. There will be resentment, anger and bitterness towards his parents. There also will be real anger and resentment towards the social workers and welfare agencies for breaking up his home. His foster parents will get some of this anger and resentment, as well. They want him to call them "mom and dad," but he will have nothing to do with that. He is far too angry to think kindly of anybody.

As if churning rage and resentment are not enough, the separated child begins to wonder why he was abandoned. "Why do I have to live in some stranger's house, when other kids live at home? Why has this happened? Maybe there is something wrong with me." This triggers self-doubt and he lays a guilt-trip on himself. On top of his other problems, he now develops a low self-image. "I'm no good, that's why this happened. If I was worth anything, my parents would have kept me." Depression often sets in at this point.

PROBLEMS WITH BEHAVIOR

There comes a time when the separated child can no longer keep this anger and resentment inside. It is uncontrollable. He has to let it out. This is where behavior problems develop, as in the case of the minister's adopted son at the beginning of this chapter. Research shows that they may crop up in one or more of nine different ways. Let's use a fictional character named Pete as an example.

Attention-Getting Actions

As a foster child, Pete is not getting the same kind of attention as the natural-born children in the home. Yet he craves for someone to take an active interest in him. His only choice is to do something that will get the attention he needs. Usually this is negative behavior, because he knows if he behaves properly, no one will notice him.

Most problems in school develop for this reason. Pete starts shooting spit-balls around the classroom. He doesn't care if the teacher sees him or not. In fact, he hopes he will be caught. The others don't want to sit in the corner, but Pete welcomes the chance. He sits there smirking. The whole class has noticed him, and so has the teacher. This is what he was after.

Picky Eating or Hoarding Food

Another problem that often develops has to do with food. Some separated children are picky eaters, while others like to hide food away. This usually happens because the child is feeling very insecure. He is away from his parents, and he wonders who will take care of him, especially if he has been moved around several times.

Pete is reacting differently. He's a picky eater. Because of the anger and resentment he feels, Pete's digestive system is not working well. Anger in any situation often has this affect. Only while he is sleeping can his food be taken care of properly, because then he is out of touch with his anger. When Pete gets up in the morning, he's hungry. He eats a good breakfast, then he goes off to school. By this time, he is reminded of something at home. Right away anger and resentment begin churning inside him and his digestive process stops. His breakfast just sits there because he is not hungry.

At lunch time, Pete sits down at the table, but he can't eat. This upsets his foster mother. "You've got to eat. You're going to sit there until you clean up your plate," she says. So he forces that lunch down on top of his breakfast, which makes him even angrier. All afternoon, he is boiling inside. So far, his digestive system has not touched either meal.

Now it is supper time, and he has quite a problem. Both foster parents insist he must eat, but he isn't the slightest bit hungry. All he can do is pick at things on his plate. If his foster parents knew how he felt, they would lay off and quit force-feeding him.

Stealing

A third reaction to his anger and resentment is the urge to steal. This is very common with separated children of all kinds. It starts small and continues to grow. First, it is a few coins from the counter, a pencil from someone's desk, or a favorite toy from his foster brother. Before long, Pete begins taking candy at the store. The older he gets, the bigger the objects he steals.

Running Away

All separated children dream of running away and most try it. Usually, they have no idea where their parents live, but this does not stop them. In those six years I spent in Indian boarding schools, I ran away four times. The first time, when I was about seven, it took us several days to find my dad. Because I was the youngest, my brothers made me knock on the door. When Dad looked out into the darkness and saw me, he nearly fell over. I think he was glad to see us, but he still made us go back to school. In other cases, the police or some motorist will pick up the runaway and bring him back.

Dropping Out of School

As the separated child grows older, his problems multiply. The anger and resentment have used up so much of his energy, his learning capacity has been affected. This makes school another burden he has to bear. A good example would be a child who has recently lost a parent or a brother or sister. In most cases, this child's grades will drop. A woman in one of my seminars shared that when her parents divorced, it took her two years before she stopped getting Ds and Fs in school.

Faced with this situation, many separated children skip school and later drop out altogether. This often happens in the second year of high school.

Breaking and Entering

What started as "borrowing" little things around the house or from unsuspecting classmates, later becomes breaking and entering. With little or no happiness in the foster home, many hours are spent with friends just hanging around. Empty homes and stores are an easy target and provide pocket money for movies and fast food.

Car Theft

One step up the scale from breaking and entering is stealing cars. The urge to have a joy ride or to get to a party in a neighboring town seems worth the risk. An accident is often involved, and the separated teen is almost always caught. The result is usually confinement of some sort.

I talked with one counselor from a large state prison in the north central part of the U.S. A big percentage of the inmates were native, so I asked him to find out how many were separated from their homes as children. He reported back to me some time later. After talking personally with each native inmate, he discovered they all were at one time separated children.

Impulsive Behavior

One trademark of many children and teens who have been removed from their homes is unexpected, unplanned, impulsive behavior. A dog may come by when they are walking down the street and they will kick it for no reason. They may smash a toy or slash the seats in a bus or restaurant. Throwing stones at birds and through windows is another common practice. This behavior is always destructive because it comes from the anger that is boiling away inside them. It is not something that is thought out ahead of time; it just happens.

Violence Towards Self

With no sense of self-worth, and a burning rage and resentment inside, many separated teens practice violence towards themselves. You will see it when they drive at high speeds and take corners on two wheels. They know they are putting their own lives in jeopardy, but that is what it's all about. Their boiling anger has been directed at themselves. "There's something wrong with me because I was taken from my parents. I'm not good like other kids." Quite often, these young people will be scarred up around their wrists and ribs from suicide attempts. To this point, they may have tried half-heartedly, but eventually they will be successful, if they keep trying.

PROBLEMS WITH OTHERS

With so much anger and resentment inside, it is only natural for relationships with others to be affected. Here are six of the typical problems separated children have in relating to people around them.

Violence Towards Others

In my counseling work, I found that 80 to 90 percent of the people who came for treatment had been through an early childhood separation. We often discussed these things in group sessions and even one-on-one in my office. One of the problems that came up most often was fighting or violence towards others. A typical conversation might go like this.

"Well, Jim, did you get in a lot of fights when you were younger, and do you still fight quite a bit?"

He would think for a moment. "Yes, I fight a lot. I guess I always have, even back in school. And I still fight a lot at home and with the neighbors."

"If you think about it, how often do you suppose you had to have a good fight in order to keep feeling right?'

"Well, I'd say about three good fights a week, or something like that. Sometimes I had to be in a fight every day."

This is typical of many separated children even after they are adults.

Abuse of Sex

Another relationship problem that often arises is abuse of sex or the inability to be satisfied sexually. This affects both boys and girls. It becomes a vicious circle that carries over generation to generation.

Between the ages of twelve and thirteen, socializing begins. It is also at this age that alcohol and drug use starts. Careless, casual sex is a natural outcome. Before long, this leads to a live-in situation. Since they are not allowed to live as a couple in the foster home, they run away, either to his home or her home. These days, many parents have no problem with this, and they let the young couple move in together. At this point, they are both school drop-outs and probably have a drug problem. Neither one has a job, and they often are in no condition to get one.

This relationship usually lasts until the girl gets pregnant. Since the young father is not able or ready to handle parenthood, he deserts the girl. She is now alone and very angry. A lot of thought is given to abortion and suicide, but in the end she decides to give birth. By this time, in an effort to handle the hurt, rage and grief she is feeling, she is a confirmed alcoholic and drug user.

With an extra mouth to feed, she suddenly discovers her lack of education is a major problem. No one will give her a job. Not knowing what else to do, she calls in the social worker and gives up her baby. Now this youngster becomes an unwanted child. She will be filled with a lot of resentment towards her mother for giving her up and towards her father for running off on them. All the things her mother went through, she will go through, and it becomes a vicious circle. By this time, they are into the third generation of separation.

No longer having a child to care for, the young mother makes the rounds of the bars. There is no shortage of men to buy the booze she wants. After a while, one of them moves in with her. They stay together until she gets pregnant, then he kicks her out or she moves on.

Meanwhile, the young father continues drinking. He meets another girl. The live together until she becomes pregnant. He moves on, meets another girl, and the story continues. No permanent relationship develops for either of them. The only things that grow are their addiction problems, their rage, and more problem children.

Distrust of People

Another common development among separated children is a distrust of people. The constant moving from home to home and their many bad experiences have left them bitter and suspicious. Having been burned several times by live-in mates, they have no faith in anybody. After all, if they can't trust their own parents, there probably isn't anyone in the whole world who can be trusted.

The principle of basic trust is gradually developed in a child from infancy. He first learns to trust an imperfect mother, then an imperfect father, and imperfect brothers and sisters. Slowly the circle widens to include other relatives, neighbors, teachers, clergy, and eventually the people of the world. Between the ages of six and twelve is when the child's value system is developed. For this the most important figure is his father. The separated child misses out on this. During those crucial years, he is moving around in foster homes with no role model he feels he can follow. When he finally reaches age thirteen, he is shaped by his peer group, and it is often made up of the "outlaws" of the community. This is where his values are usually set.

Too Strong an Attachment to One Person

Everyone needs someone to trust. In a desperate effort to satisfy this craving, a separated child will often form an attachment with one person that is much too strong. It is usually with some other child in similar circumstances. There is a sort of mutual drawing together, but they become very anti-social. Instead of associating with other people, they would rather withdraw and stay by themselves.

Striking Out Against Authority

Authority is a bad word with most separated children since it was the authorities who took them from their homes. This is reflected in their attitude towards law and order. Personal and property rights mean nothing, because they feel they have been deprived of these themselves. When foster parents start laying down rules, the natural reaction is "Who are you to tell me what to do?" Church rules and the ultimate authority of God are also ignored. Since God allowed their lives to be messed up like this, then they want nothing to do with Him. Working with an employer also becomes a problem because here again they are faced with authority. Being unable to accept the directives of the one who pays the wages means unhappy work experiences and frequent job changes.

Need to Cling

Many separated children have a craving for intimacy. All their lives they have wanted to be loved and cuddled by a family where they felt they belonged. Since they have not found this, whenever the opportunity arises, they will cling to another person. This need is also reflected in their abuse of sex and their unusually strong attachment to one special friend.

PROBLEMS WITH ALCOHOL AND DRUG ABUSE

By the time the foster child reaches the teenage years, he often begins to drink and use drugs. Since this is largely in response to the anger and resentment within, alcohol and drug abuse becomes a way of life. Unless treatment is given, they will many times die with these problems unresolved. As has already been mentioned, 80 to 90 percent of the people in treatment, and an even higher percentage of prison inmates, were at one time separated children. In the case of the inmates, most were convicted for crimes they committed while either drunk or high on drugs.

PROBLEMS WITH EMOTIONS

The whole emotional life of the separated child is filled largely with negative feelings. There is anger and rage for the situation in which they find themselves. Day by day, they walk around under a cloud of fear, anxiety, worry and insecurity. Loneliness and rejection become a way of life for them. A large measure of depression and emotional pain leads to bitterness and spiritual wounding.

This is far removed from the emotional life of the average child still at home with his birth parents. For most such children, life is care-free and secure. They get up on a Saturday morning and eat their breakfast. "Mom, a bunch of us are going down to the park to play for a while."

"Okay, dear. You be careful, and make sure you're home for dinner."

After dinner, they are off again. On their way out the door, they yell, "Mom, we're going swimming this afternoon."

Mom says, "That's fine, dear. Watch out now and be sure there are others kids in the water with you. See you at supper."

That is the way it is with most children, but not with those who are separated. The emotional turmoil they go through practically drives them to drink. No one recognizes their needs; no therapy is offered. Instead they are branded as juvenile delinquents, vandals, beyond hope. Many times negative comments are made that make the problems even worse. "You'll never amount to anything." "You're going to be just like your mom and dad." Not only is this damaging to the self-images of these troubled youngsters, but it also serves as a self-fulfilling prophesy. "Okay, if that's what you think I am, then that's exactly what I'm going to be." With so many strokes against them, these children need as much help as they can get. Unfortunately, for the most part, nobody gives them a chance.

PROBLEMS WITH MENTAL PROCESSES

A final area in which separated children develop problems is that of mental processes. If we stop and think about it for a moment, we would realize this should be expected. As humans, we are emotional creatures. When our emotions are in turmoil, nothing else works right. For example, a student is filled with anxiety. His future depends on the results of the final examination. The question sheets are handed out. The clock begins ticking, and suddenly, there is a total mental block. Several days of round-the-clock cramming has left him so tense his mind blanks out. This is how we are made. Imagine then what problems separated children must face. Certainly no one has more emotional turmoil than they do. As a result, this inner chaos frequently causes difficulties at school and with basic mental processes. We will look briefly at three typical problems.

Short Attention Spans

With so much emotional unrest, separated children often have very short attention spans. They try to listen, but their minds keep drifting off. It becomes very difficult for them to concentrate for more than a short while. Their personal problems compete for attention with the voice of the teacher. By the end of classes, they have only bits and pieces of the information they need. Key parts that tie it all together were missed. The natural result of this problem is failing grades.

Learning Disabilities

Another problem that often crops up is that of learning disabilities. Most often, these are in the areas of reading, arithmetic and the ability to work with ideas. There are several reasons for this. With no concerned, loving parent to talk with him and read to him, words and ideas are often new when the separated child first comes to school. This puts him at an immediate disadvantage. When it comes to remedial work and extra help at home, again the loving parent who takes a personal interest is missing. Then, too, the constant shifting from one home to another usually means changing schools as well. This is never easy for any child, but is especially difficult for separated children. They face again and again the social hurdles of new teachers, new classmates, new home, new community, and finding new friends. Having to change schools during the school years also means whole units of work may be missed. Since our education system builds block upon block, new learning is shaky because foundational blocks of information are missing. This adds a further handicap.

I have seen very real evidence of this in reading numerous native newspapers. Often there is a call for native foster parents. To encourage response, one or more children who need immediate care may be featured, complete with a photo and a brief biography. In reading through these notices, I invariably see comments about being below grade level, needing extra help with studies, and requiring special education. Granted, some of these problems may reflect the child's biological make-up, but a large percentage of them are due to his environment and not his intellect.

Poor Self-Image

The separated child is his own worst critic. No one thinks less of him than he does himself. He considers himself inferior because he thinks that is why his parents rejected him. The constant shifting from home to home tells him others don't want him either. Learning problems at school tell him he is stupid. In most cases, these are wrong conclusions, but the child firmly believes them.

With this understanding of himself, he will face severe limitations for the rest of his life. Because he thinks he is stupid, he is going to drop out of school. With poor education, the kinds of jobs he qualifies for are limited. Most will be very low paying. Such an attitude also determines the kind of mate he will choose, the kind of home he establishes, the method for rearing his children and the kinds of friends he chooses.

From my experience, I would say at least half our Indian people have a very poor self-image and I know it is not justified. I remember the days when we were in residential school. There were a lot of very talented young people there. Some were natural artists. They could draw some pictures that had me spell-bound when I looked at them. And they were musicians, too. We had a real talented band. Man, we were so proud of that bunch when they played. We used to sit and listen to them at basketball games, and they were good! I don't think Indian people were cut out to be losers at all. If it wasn't for this problem with self-image, I know a lot of our people would be doctors and lawyers and very successful business persons. Unfortunately, so many are handicapped by this poor self-image, and doubly so for those who are, or were, separated children.

I remember when a psychologist and I shared this material with a group of teenagers on one U.S. reservation. For about five or six months, we set forth these ideas in a classroom setting. They seemed interested, but we had no idea how well they were identifying until the beginning of one of the later classes. One day when we came in ready to teach, the class stopped us. "Before you start," they said, "we want to share with you something that we found out about our village."

"Okay, go ahead," we said.

One of them spoke for the group. "Well, first of

all, we find that there are two peer groups here. The one we belong to is made up of kids that come from broken homes, like we have been talking about. We all seem to have the same kinds of problems. We drop out of school. We're on probation or we're having problems with the law. We're into drugs and alcohol. And we're not getting along with the people in the village. We're always in trouble."

I was impressed. "Sounds like you've been doing some hard thinking," I said. "You've really been using your heads."

"But wait, that isn't all. We've also been thinking about that other peer group. They come from families that are still together. They are not dropping out of school like we are. Those kids are finishing high school and some of them are going on to get further training. They may come in and try alcohol and drugs once or twice with us, but then they leave it alone. They don't get hooked like we do. They don't get in trouble with the law. I don't think any of them are on probation, and they get along fine with the rest of the people in the village, not like us."

I was pretty excited by what I was hearing. These teenagers were finding help for the problems they faced.

A year later, I met the local counsellor and I asked her about these separated teens. "Art, it's an amazing thing," she said. "That money we spent on those seminars with you guys was some of the best money we ever spent! Those kids are still on the ball."

This chapter has covered some stark, frightening material. The situation facing separated children is not pretty, but I feel strongly that it can be changed. If we can bring them to an understanding of the problems they face and the reasons why, then the battle is half won. The next step is to give them concrete help in dealing with the anger and rejection that dominates their lives. The last chapter in this book is dedicated to this purpose.

CHAPTER TEN

Help For Separated Children

THE LAST CHAPTER dealt with some of the painful problems faced by separated children, problems like the ones I faced and even worse. And the chapters before that touched on other aspects of unresolved grief that are destroying our Indian people. With this as background, let's now consider a few suggestions for dealing with these problems. While much of what I am going to share refers directly to childhood separation, a number of these ideas also will help with other types of grieving problems.

I realize many good counsellors base their advice on a background in psychology, but I prefer to use the spiritual approach. People don't need to know how to cope with their problems, as much as they need help in facing and eliminating them. By using the basic principles of scripture, I feel a spiritual approach can do exactly this. I have seen its effectiveness both in my own life and in others.

Forgiveness, for example, is a spiritual principle that most hurting people need to know about in order to handle their grief and anger. Without forgiveness, most of them will carry their pain with them to the grave. This came close to happening in my life.

It was not until I was around sixty years old that I got in touch with my own feelings on the issue of childhood separation. At the time, I was working at an Indian residential treatment center in Minnesota. As I counseled hundreds of native people and sat in on different workshops, I slowly became aware of the problems faced by children who lived apart from their parents. Then I started asking myself some questions. Was I just like them? For six crucial years of my life I was separated from my mother and father. Did I have any of this anger and these feelings of resentment? I realized at once that I did. As an early teenager drinking got a serious hold on me, and my brothers and I were some of the biggest thieves in a two-county area. Everything about us showed anger striking out. Our lives fitted the description of a separated child to a "T."

As I thought further about those years of growing up without my parents, I began to understand my own feelings a lot better. Until that point, I didn't know why I carried resentment against my mother. It suddenly became very clear. From the day she tricked us into getting on that train, I had felt betrayed. I was only six at the time, and I cried non-stop for the first three weeks of school. This was followed by six years of almost no contact with my parents. Then when we finally got back home, we discovered our mother had also abandoned our dad and was married to another man. This upset us even more.

As I came to understand these feelings of resentment, I knew I had to deal with them. By this time, my mother had already passed away, so I went out to her grave. There I confessed the resentment and bitterness I had toward her all those years. I talked out loud as though she could hear me until I felt I had cleared out my system of all the bad feelings. At last, I could forgive her.

The hurt of those days is gone since I dealt with it, and now I have some good, fond memories of her. Today, if she were alive, I could put my arm around her and honestly say, "Ma, I don't know if there is a woman alive that I'd want to trade you for. I'm just glad that God gave you to me as my mother."

When a person forgives someone who has wronged him, as I did with my mother, the root of anger is removed and there is no longer a reason to be upset. To my thinking this is a lot better than discovering ways to control my rage for the rest of my life. I would much rather be rid of it once and for all. And as an important, vital side benefit, forgiveness builds good moral character. A person who has learned to forgive is well equipped for life to handle all of the painful situations he will face. Whenever he is wronged or he suffers a major loss, instead of letting the rage boil inside until it destroys him, he will be able to forgive and get on with productive living.

USING THE SPIRITUAL APPROACH

Based on my own experience and from reading published reports, I would estimate that half the population of most native communities have had some experience with separation in their childhood. Countless others are battling with unresolved grief. If such is the case, this presents a great opportunity to put this spiritual approach to work. In so doing, here are several steps you may want to follow.

Understand the Problem of Separation

The first step in helping a separated person is to understand what separation is all about. This means getting to know the theory, as well as the impact of the problem in the community.

1. Separation in Theory. An excellent way to understand what it means to be a separated person is to read and re-read chapter nine of this book. It discusses the problems of the separated child. Until you can grasp the situation as one of these children sees it, you will not be ready to help someone deal with it. You also may want to do further reading on certain aspects of the problem. Though very little is actually written on the separated child, most city and regional libraries should have something on related subjects, as should university and commercial bookstores.

2. Separation in Your Community. Once you understand what separation does to a person, you need to find out how it has affected your community. A phone call or visit to your regional office for Indian Affairs could provide a wealth of information. Copies of local surveys, statistics and reports also would help you get a handle on the problem in your area. Then make an appointment with the local social worker or the supervisor. They can explain how separations are handled and what policies are currently in effect.

The older people in the community are another terrific resource. They can give you details you will find no place else. Ask them about tragic, unexpected deaths in the area, and what happened to the family members who were left. Chances are you will begin to detect unresolved grieving problems.

By talking to the older people, you will also be able to gather information on families which have broken up and whose children have gone into adoptive or foster homes. Here and there you will discover several generations of separated children. Unable to resolve their own rage and resentment over disrupted childhoods, they unknowingly are passing the problem down to children and grandchildren.

After you have gathered the information, make a list of all the families, noting the facts you have learned. As you do, you will begin to see your community in a new light, and you will have a base from which you can begin to make a significant impact. When you know the pain they are suffering, the compassion will follow.

Share the Understanding You Have Gained

Knowledge of this kind must be shared if it is going to help, but first you must take every precaution to protect personal privacy. One of the first places where you should share your findings is in a meeting with the tribal or band leaders. You need to explain your research to them and what you would like to do with it. Then with their approval, begin to use every opportunity you can to make it known.

Since you are dealing with problems that disrupt and destroy lives and communities, the social workers need to know what you have discovered. You also may want to explore the possibility of leading a discussion at a parent-teachers meeting. Informal conversation over coffee is another way to let people know about the roots of some very common problems. If you are a clergyman or lay minister, try speaking several times a year on grief and separation. By using a positive approach, rather than condemnation, and by stating clearly your willingness to understand and help, you might be surprised at the response you will get. Perhaps you could host a workshop on this subject. In the seminars I have offered, most people welcomed input in these difficult areas.

Develop Trust Relationships

As community members become more aware of the problems faced by separated children, individuals here and there will begin to identify personal needs. This is your cue. Do what you can to develop trust relationships with these individuals. Once they feel comfortable with you, you will then be in a position to help them work through their problems. But be patient. This is not something that happens over night.

Watch for crisis moments that develop—a serious accident, the loss of a loved one, hospitalization, an arrest, or repeated drunken-driving charges. When people are faced with difficult moments like this, they are often more open for discussion of personal problems and are looking for solutions. Pray for the right opportunities, and when they come, be ready.

Another excellent source of contacts would be an open AA or Al-Anon meeting. These people know they have problems and will probably be more than interested in learning about your findings. A few questions to the group about separated childhoods and tragic, unexpected deaths will either confirm or deny the truth of your information.

Some of the people who need help the most may seem to be the most unlikely. Don't let this fool you. The wildest bunch of teenagers, deep into drugs, alcohol, vandalism and sex, could well be separated children expressing their anger, resentment and hurt. Others with similar needs could be the parents of these teenagers, their grandparents, the local drunk, the woman or man who can't find a lasting relationship, or someone in tribal leadership.

Age and station in life are no barrier to the problems of separation and grief. Someone told me of a grown man who still hated his father because of childhood separation. He said, "All these years I've hated my dad because when the BIA came to take me away to school, he stood in the door of our home and waved good-bye. I wanted him to stop them, but he didn't and I hated him for it. I just realized now that there was nothing he could do." This man spent a large part of his life feeling forsaken, when in fact his father cared very deeply for him.

My mother is another example. She died at age eighty-nine still suffering from childhood separations, and she passed these problems on to me and my brothers. When I was sent away to school, my mother never really had a chance to show me love. So I grew up, married and had children without knowing how to show them love and affection. It was absolutely foreign to me.

I was talking to my aunt about this one day, and she said, "Art, don't be too hard on your mother. You don't know what we went through. Your mother and I also were separated kids. We were shipped off to a government school for a lot longer than you were. By the time we got out, we were young women already. Your mother was never given a chance to know love, and that's why she could never offer it. She never learned how."

My mother needed someone to build a trust relationship with her to help her work out the problems of her childhood separation, but no one came. I needed the same kind of help, but didn't get it, and look at the hellish kind of life I went through before I got straightened out. There are a lot of our native people who can be spared this experience if we can get to them at the right moment with the right message. But the key is friendship and trust. They will only accept it from a friend in whom they have confidence.

Build a Biblical Self-Image

A poor self-image is a problem most Indians face, but particularly those who were, or are, separated children. Often, it is also a major problem for the spouse and children of an alcoholic. After living with physical and verbal abuse over a long period of time, they begin to believe the negative things they hear about themselves. And of course, the alcoholics rate very poorly in their own eyes.

A poor self-image is a tremendous burden for anyone to carry because it automatically programs a person for failure. As long as somebody feels he is worthless, he will spend his life proving himself right. This is the story of far too many of our people across the continent, and it's destroying them. They desperately need help in weeding out this life-crippling attitude. And I believe here is one place where the spiritual approach shines, for it introduces God into the situation. Not only does it give us His view on the matter, but it also opens the way for divine help in changing for the better.

I remember a discussion with a man who came to talk with me about a problem his daughter had with low self-image. The father was quite disturbed.

"Art, I don't know what to do about our daughter," he said. "She's so down on herself, I'm afraid for her. She's quit school and she is always talking about suicide. If we don't get some help, one of these days she's going to do it."

I knew he was desperate, so we talked for quite a while about his daughter and the problem of low self-image. The information I shared with him is what I am going to share here.

Low self-image usually begins in the home, especially if one of the parents is an alcoholic. To cover for his own feelings of worthlessness, the drinking person blames others for his problems. There will be a lot of put-downs, a lot of blaming and name-calling. As the children listen to this over a period of time, they begin to believe what they hear. They grow to see themselves as being stupid, unable to succeed, and all-around failures. Eventually, many threaten suicide and some attempt it.

Once a person develops a low self-image, it often affects his whole life. The lower his opinion of himself, the less schooling he is going to get. Both his lack of education and his self-image will determine the kinds of jobs he will have and the size of his income. Very few positions will be open to him, and the ones that are will often be seasonal. Later, his self-image will determine the kind of spouse he will select. If he considers himself to be on the bottom of the social ladder, then he is going to look for a spouse who is also at the bottom. He will never select one above what he thinks himself to be.

Self-image will also be reflected in the place where he lives. A person with a low self-image likely will never buy a home. His residence will usually be in the low-rental or slum areas of the community. The kinds of friends he chooses will have the same kind of low self-image and will often be of the skid-row type. Also affected will be the manner in which he rears his children. What started off as verbal abuse in the home thus has ended up shaping the whole life of the child.

As I was growing up, I experienced a lot of what I have just talked about in general terms. For example, when I would help my mother with the dishes and happened to drop one, she would tell me to be more careful.

Then pretty soon, there would be another bang as a second dish hit the floor. That's when mother would blow up. "Art, can't you do anything right? I don't think you could even sweep the floor right. What's the matter with you? You're going to be just like your dad —lazy and good for nothing." I didn't agree with what she said about dad, but after I heard her description of me a few times, I began to believe I was just like she said I was.

There was another problem in our family that caused all of my brothers and me to develop a very low self-image. My mother had been married once, before she married our dad. She had one son by that first marriage, and then she lost that husband in a hunting accident. I doubt if my mother ever recovered from the loss of that mate. She never did her grief work. Thus her oldest boy was Number One and the rest of us were second class citizens. When we were treated and spoken to in this way, we eventually accepted mother's angry words as facts.

Then when we moved over to our grandmother's home, we faced a similar problem. My aunt had passed away and left a baby boy. After the father abandoned him, my grandparents raised the baby as their own. This boy was treated as Number One, and again my brothers and I were second class citizens. This happened in a third situation when we went off to schools in the community. This time it was white people who were Number One and we were second class because we were Indians. I, for one, carried this burden for many years until I finally learned how to deal with it using spiritual principles.

Serve Your Way to Greatness

To give you an idea of how I might help someone work at improving his self-image and life-style, let me tell you about someone I will call Agnes. The court sent her for treatment and she dropped into my office for counseling one day. We talked a bit to get acquainted and I learned she had five children. Each one was from a different father.

As we discussed this situation and some of her other problems, she admitted how unhappy she was. "I don't like living like this, but how do I get out of it?" she said. "These men can't be trusted. They promise to marry me, but when they see somebody they like better, they run off. And there I am stuck with another baby. I guess I'm just no good."

"The problem is not that you're no good," I said. "The problem is because of the kind of life you are living. You want a husband, so you go drinking in the bars to meet one. But most of the men who go there are looking for a woman to sleep with, not a wife. When you go out with them, they are thinking sex rather than marriage. If you want to find a worthwhile husband, you will have to begin looking in a different place. And you will need to become the kind of woman this man would want to raise his children."

At this point, I began to explain to her how to change her own self-image and the way others saw her. If she would do this, I told her, with God's help, she could become the kind of person any decent man would want for a life-time companion and to be the mother of their children.

Since Agnes had such a problem with a poor self-image, I began with scripture. "In Genesis, the first book of the Bible, we are told that we were created in the image of God. This is the basis for feeling good about ourselves, for if we are patterned after our Creator, we must be something worthwhile. Using God as our pattern, let's get to know what He is like so we can be more like Him.

"First of all, God is perfect and He is 100 percent great. When we stop to compare ourselves to Him and think about being like Him, it seems impossible. We don't have the talent or ability to rise to a level of any kind of greatness. But this is only human thinking.

From God's point of view, greatness is measured by how much we are willing to serve, not by how many people serve us. Jesus was a perfect example. He came to this world to serve people, not to be served. By the way He lived and the things He did, He made the role of a servant important. He says that any person who wants to become great must serve others. And the one who wants to become the greatest of all must become servant of all.

"This puts greatness within the reach of everyone because anybody and everybody can be a servant. If you want to develop a good self-image, if you want to become great, begin to serve other people. Help those who have needs. Start by being a good employee. Work for your boss as if you were working for God. Then watch for other people and other ways you can serve. This is the path to greatness."

Many people think of a dictator in some wealthy country when they think of greatness, but they are mistaken. I was in Italy when Mussolini was caught and executed during World War II. As soon as people heard the news, there was dancing in the streets and rejoicing. They celebrated his death. And the same was true when Hitler killed himself. The whole world was happy.

It was a different story, however, with England's Prime Minister Churchill for he served people instead of abusing them. He was wealthy and had a lot of business concerns when he became prime minister, but he set these aside to serve the millions of people for whom he was now responsible. This man made decisions daily that involved the lives of millions of men. And the day he died, I got a lump in my throat. I mourned along with the rest of the world because he was one of earth's really great statesmen. Because he served those under his authority, he was great in the eyes of the world.

I think it would be well for any person in business to know that when he is placed in authority he is to be the servant of everyone under him. This principle is good for husbands as the head of their families, as well. He is not to be a dictator over his wife and children, but their servant. The more we all learn to serve, the greater we become in the eyes of those we help.

Develop the Quality of Goodness

As Agnes and I talked further, I introduced her to a second pattern that God sets for us which is goodness. "God is not only 100 percent perfect and great, but He is also 100 percent good," I told her. "All good comes from Him. Because we are created in His image, this means we are capable of goodness, too. Paul wrote that we are the workmanship of God, created for good works (Ephesians 2:10). He also wrote, 'We know that God makes all things work together for the good of those who love Him and are chosen to be a part of His plan. God knew from the beginning who would put their trust in Him. So He chose them and made them to be like His Son' (Romans 8:28, 29).

"This last verse talks about the person who loves the Lord and has put his life under God's authority to be a good servant of the Lord Jesus Christ. As we do this, God's plan for us is to be made more and more like Jesus Himself. And what was Jesus like? He was good —without sin, the Bible says—and He was a servant, and He expects us to be good and to become good servants, too.

"Now it is one thing to expect us to be good, but it's another thing to actually be good. God knew this and He made it possible. Once we have accepted Him as our Savior and have invited the Holy Spirit into our lives, then the fruit of the Spirit (Galatians 5:22) has been planted as a seed in our hearts. Out of this will grow love, joy, peace, patience, goodness, kindness, gentleness, self-control and faithfulness.

"Anyone who starts to develop these fruits will begin to notice changes taking place. Family members will notice, too. They will start making comments like, 'You're really different lately. You haven't been hollering at us for a long time now, and we like that. And you're patient with us. It was hard for us to accept at first, but now we see that you've really changed and we're glad.'

"As we work at developing these fruits, we will see a change at our place of employment, too. By being totally honest with God, ourselves and everyone else, people will see the difference. We will soon be in line for promotions and pay raises. When someone retires, the boss will be looking for people with good, solid character, and those he can trust are going to be considered.

"Developing the fruit of the Spirit will end up changing our whole lives. We will be better off financially because we won't be wasting our money on expensive, harmful habits. And we will be healthier, because there is something healing about the fruit of the Spirit. Letting love, peace and forgiveness grow, along with the other fruit, mends deep wounds and injuries. These are all side benefits that come to us as we begin to work ourselves out of this low self-image.

"As this fruit of the Spirit grows in our lives, we will slowly change our attitude about ourselves, and our whole lifestyle will change as well. Instead of the old person who sees himself as worthless, there will be a new person who is honest, humble, and understanding, a person who is grateful, forgiving and gentle. The "new" person, if he is unmarried, now will begin looking for someone with these same qualities. When he gets his increases in pay, one day he will move out of the low-rent district and into better housing. He may even think about buying his own home. And he will be finding new friends, for he will be going to church now and there will be others there who also are working at developing the fruit of the Spirit in their lives. In this way everything is going to change for that person as he begins to build a good self-image based on spiritual, scriptural principles. I have found no other way that brings lasting results."

Explain God's Special Interest in Separated People

Most of the suggestions I have made so far in this chapter will help with a wide range of problems, but this last section deals particularly with those who are hurting·from a childhood separation. In dealing with this problem, there are two verses I feel are of prime importance. The first is found in Isaiah 49:15. The Lord is talking and He says, "Can a woman forget her nursing child? Can she have no pity on the son to whom she gave birth? Even these may forget, but I will not forget you."

The second verse is Psalm 27:10. The Psalmist says, "When my father and my mother forsake me, then the Lord will take me up" (KJV). Another version says, "For my father and my mother have left me. But the Lord will take care of me." This is the kind of good news that every separated child needs to hear. God says very clearly that He has a special interest in abandoned children. Their parents may forget them, but God won't. And not only will He remember them, but He also will pick them up and take care of them.

As I thought about these promises from the Word of God, my mind was drawn to a number of Bible children who also were separated from their parents. Right away, I began studying the Word to see how God dealt with them. What I discovered amazed me. God not only remembered each one, as He promised, but He also picked them up and made something special out of their lives. Each one became an outstanding person of his day, and most are classed among the significant leaders of all time. Their stories are something every separated child needs to hear, even those who are now senior citizens. What God did for these Bible kids, He also wants to do for those of us who grew up without our parents.

Moses, An Adopted Child

The first separated child that I remembered from the Bible was Moses (Exodus 1-5). The Egyptian law said he was supposed to be killed, but his parents hid him away as long as they could. Then they placed him in a basket made with bulrushes and set him afloat in the quiet water at the edge of the Nile River. His sister Miriam stayed to watch over him.

Things were fine for a while, until their secret was discovered. When the Pharoah's daughter and her servants came down to bathe, they saw the basket. One of the maids brought it to the princess, and when she saw the baby Moses, she wanted to rear him as her own child. Now that was some foster mother—the daughter of the country's top ruler! But how would he survive? He still needed his mother's milk.

At this point, Miriam could keep quiet no longer. She stepped out of hiding and approached the princess. "If you like, I will find you someone who can nurse the baby for you. Then when he is old enough to eat regular food, we will bring him to the palace," she said.

The princess was delighted, and Miriam took baby Moses home to his own mother. The day finally came, however, for Moses to be separated from his parents, and he went to live with the daughter of the Pharoah. There was no other choice. It was either the palace or death. The parents understood that, but did the little boy?

The years passed. Moses became a young man. He had everything he could ever want, except his parents and his home. Did it affect him? Yes, I believe it did. I don't think it was just social justice that fanned the flame of his anger that day when he killed the Egyptian. I think he was lashing out at the whole Egyptian nation for taking him from his family, a typical reaction for a separated child.

We jump ahead now in Moses' story to the time of the burning bush (Exodus 3, 4). True to His word, the Lord remembered the separated child in a special way—He spoke to him out of the bush and gave him a very important job to do.

What was Moses' reaction to God's call? "I can't do

it. They won't listen to me. They don't remember who You are. And besides, I'm no good at speaking in public.'' How is that for a self-image? It sounds to me like Moses did not think very much of himself, another typical reaction of a separated child.

Once the Lord convinced Moses he could do it, and promised to help him, we see a very different man. Moses, filled with anger and resentment, insecurity and doubt from his childhood, suddenly becomes a leader who makes his mark on history. Though he missed out on the blessings of growing up with his parents, God stepped into the picture and more than made up the difference. "When my father and my mother forsake me, then the Lord will take me up.''

Samuel, A Foster Child

Samuel was another separated child (I Samuel 1 - 3). He knew who his parents were, and had contact with them once a year, but he couldn't live with them. Can you imagine how he felt when he saw his parents leaving him behind? I am sure some of the typical thoughts of a separated child ran through his mind. "Why can't I go home with them? Don't they love me enough to take me along? There must be something wrong with me and that's why they don't want me.''

From the age of four on, his foster parents were Eli, the high priest, and Eli's wife. Samuel was in a religious setting, but the place was not very godly. Eli's sons were sleeping with different women right there in the Temple and many other sinful things were happening.

It was not the best place for a young boy to grow up, but God had His eye on him. He gave Samuel a heart that wanted to do right. And when the proper time came, the Lord put a special call on his life. He had an important job for this separated child to do. Samuel became the greatest prophet of them all. He was also a priest and a judge of the nation of Israel. History records the story of his leadership. God did with him just as He promised. He picked him up and used him to make a godly impact on a whole nation.

Esther, A Fearful Teenager

God's call is not limited to boys and men. His promises are for everyone including separated girls. Esther is a good example. As a child, she lost her parents. The Bible doesn't say how, but it does say she was reared by her cousin, Mordecai. The story of her life is recorded in a book of the Bible which is named after her. It reveals a young woman who is fearful and unsure of herself, and yet who becomes queen of the Persian empire. With God's help, she faced a crisis that could have meant certain death for her, and came out a winner. By her courage, she saved the whole nation of Israel from destruction. That is some record of accomplishment for a separated child, and the Lord made it possible as He promised.

Can you see in that story some parallels that a separated teenage girl needs to know? Many are shy and fearful, craving love and security just like Esther. God doesn't love one person any more than another. Just as He met this young Jewish girl's needs, He is ready to supply the needs of today's separated children. God's blessings are there for everyone who will trust and obey him.

Joseph, A Troubled Orphan

The story of Joseph is another tale of tragedy and triumph. His mother Rachel died when he was young, so here we have a grieving situation. He still had his father Jacob, but the women who raised him were his Aunt Leah and two maids. Jacob fathered many other children from these women, but Joseph and his baby brother, Benjamin, were semi-orphans in the home. They were the only ones without a mother. To make matters worse, the other children hated Joseph, and finally sold him into slavery in Egypt.

This should have given him ample reason to be turned off on society like most separated native children. Nobody would have questioned it if he had said, "Just wait.

One day, I'm going to come back and deal with those ten brothers who did this to me. I'll get my chance, and when I do…'' A normal human reaction might have been to cry, "God, why did You sell me out like that?" and then turn his devotion to the false gods of the Egyptians. But none of this happened, and I believe the reason was because God was keeping His promise to this separated child.

The dark side of Joseph's life was not yet over. He was falsely accused of assaulting a woman, and thrown into prison. Then God began to turn his life around. He became a supervisor of other prisoners, and eventually rose to be prime minister of Egypt.

The story of his reunion with his brothers is a wonderful example of the difference God can make in the life of a separated child. None of the bitterness was shown that normally would be expected of Joseph. Instead, he took the spiritual approach and learned to forgive. In place of anger and a spirit of revenge, there was love, concern and compassion. The Lord caused this semi-orphan and former slave to be the salvation of his starving family.

Daniel, A Residential Student

When we first meet Daniel, he is a separated teenager going to school in a strange place called Babylon. It wasn't a typical Indian residential school, but he lived, learned and ate apart from his family. As far as we know, his parents may even have been dead. I think the thing that carried him through this tough time was his unfailing faith and reliance upon God. He was able to live without compromise in an ungodly environment, and eventually played a major role in the government of the land.

Here once again is a role model for separated native children in your community. When He is given a chance, the Lord steps in and gives the strength to be faithful to God and different from the others who are getting into trouble.

What God did for these who lived so long ago, He wants to do for those of us who are separated "children" today. He still promises to "pick up" anyone who will give Him a chance. Life is too short and too special to waste by carrying a burden of hurt and bitterness to the grave. We need to believe God's promise and hold Him to His word. If we let Him, the Lord can still make our lives very, very good.

CHAPTER ELEVEN

The Challenge of the Neglected

GENERALLY SPEAKING, OUR native population can be divided into two groups—the 20 percent who are successful by most standards and have relatively few difficulties, and the 80 percent who are being destroyed by major problems. To our shame, for several generations now, the church has focused its attention on the 20 percent, and has generally written off the larger group which needs help the most. Either through ignorance, frustration, or perhaps lack of specialized training, the church has considered the bulk of Indian people to be unresponsive and too difficult to reach. This is a situation I hope **The Grieving Indian** will help to change.

The Example of Jesus

When I began in the ministry, the group I worked with were the people who appeared to be trouble free and were not involved in drugs or alcohol. In those days, for some reason I trusted my own abilities and strengths to bring about the conversions of these people. Since they had the fewest problems, it seemed only logical that they would be the most likely to respond.

This was contrary to the Word of God. The teaching of Christ is that while it is impossible for men to enter the kingdom of God on their own, with God all things are possible (Matthew 19:26). Another time when He spoke to the Pharisees, Jesus said He did not come to call right-living people to repent, but troubled, sinful people (Matthew 9:13). He said it was the sick who needed a doctor, not the people who were well (Matthew 9:12). Then as I studied the early chapters of Proverbs, once again I saw that the Lord was addressing the people of the world who have problems. Through these verses and many others, I slowly came to realize that Jesus gave His attention to the "80 percent," not the smaller group.

The Testimony of "Troubled" Converts

As I look back over my ministry and that of other Indian workers, I can see now that the Lord was right. The native people who have the greatest testimony today are the grateful people who came out of that 80-percent group, the people who had real troubles. These are the ones who came off skidrow, the ones who hit bottom.

I remember two women from one of the reservations where we ministered over thirty years ago. One evening during one of our services, they came forward to pray and give their lives to Jesus. My brother and I helped them in making their decisions. Then, as we visited the homes in the days that followed, we found many of the people were laughing. "Do you know who those two were that you were praying with the other night?" they asked. "They are two of the meanest, most trouble-some, alcoholic Indians on the reservation. There is no way they are going to be able to stick with it."

There was nothing we could do about it at that point, except pray. The Lord did the rest. Those women started coming to church and kept coming very faith-fully. And now, thirty years later, I cannot say enough good about them. They have been faithful to the Lord all these years, and have done everything in their power to rear their children for God. They have the respect of everyone in the community for the way they have lived. We did not know they were part of the "80 percent," but the Lord did, and He performed a miracle in their lives.

In I Corinthians 6:9-11, the Apostle Paul said some very pointed things about the local "80 percent." He named a whole list of sinful practices the believers were to avoid. Then he concluded by saying that some of them had done these very things before they became Christians. According to Paul's own words, there were a number of people in that fellowship who were formerly part of Corinth's "80 percent." Then the early church gave them what they needed, and their lives were changed.

Unfortunately, that is not nearly so true today. Seventy-five percent of alcoholics who are now sober attribute their sobriety to AA, not the ministry of the church. I don't know how it happened, but somewhere along the line the theology and faith of the clergy—and I was one of them—no longer seems to include the possibility of transformation for alcoholics and other members of the "80 percent." This should not be. The most logical place for troubled people to find help and hope is the church. However, until the time comes that the church is ready to step out in faith and offer the assistance our people require, we need to make use of the community resources now available to help us in our ministry.

The burden of this book has come out of my years of experience. I have been on the other side of the tracks among the "80 percent." And I have been on the ministry side, too. I know what it is like to try to help troubled people without the necessary knowledge or experience. I also know what it is like to see bound people set free. My hope is that this book will help you profit from my successes, while avoiding my mistakes.

When Jesus said, "The fields are white unto harvest" (John 4:35), I am sure He had the "80 percent" in mind. A field that is ready for harvest is golden brown or tan in color, but if it is left too long, it becomes overripe and changes to white. At this stage, the slightest breeze will cause the grain to fall to the ground and be lost. No matter what a farmer does when he is harvesting a "white" field, he is going to lose a lot of grain.

The 80-percent portion of our native people are "white unto harvest." There is no way we are going to be able to reach all these people before they fall to the ground and are lost. But this is no excuse for not reaching as many as possible. Use this book to help you focus on the grieving, 80 percent. God will give the increase.

NOTES

Chapter Four

1. Arthur S. Freese, *Help For Your Grief* (New York: Schocken Books, 1977), page 21.

2. Elisabeth Kubler-Ross, *On Death And Dying* (New York: Collier Books, Macmillan Publishing Company, 1969).

3. Edgar N. Jackson, *Understanding Grief* (Nashville: Abingdon, 1957), p. 19.

4. Freese, page 70.

5. Robert Fulton, *Death and Identity* (New York: John Wiley and Sons, Inc., 1965), chapter four. This refers to a study conducted by Mervyn Shoor and Mary H. Speed.

6. Freese, p. 5.

Chapter Five

1. Arthur S. Freese, *Help For Your Grief* (New York: Schocken Books, 1977), p. 25.

2. Paul Tournier, trans. Edwin Hudson, *The Violence Within* (New York: Harper and Row Publishers, 1978), p. 111.

3. Edgar N. Jackson, *The Many Faces of Grief* (Nashville: Abingdon, 1978), p. 13.

4. Freese, page 59.

5. Bernadine Kreis and Alice Pattie, *Up From Grief* (San Francisco: Harper and Row Publishers, Inc., 1969), p. 45.

BIBLIOGRAPHY

Dunn, Jerry, with Bernard Palmer. *God Is For The Alcoholic.* Chicago: Moody Press, rev. ed. 1986. Pp. 240.

Freese, Arthur S. *Help For Your Grief.* New York: Schocken Books, Random House Publishers, 1977. Pp. 197.

Jackson, Edgar N. *The Many Faces of Grief.* Nashville: Abingdon, 1978. Pp. 174.

_____. *Understanding Grief.* Nashville: Abingdon, 1957. Pp. 255.

Kubler-Ross, Elisabeth. *On Death and Dying.* New York: Collier Books, Macmillan Publishing Co., 1969. Pp. 290.

Kreis, Bernadine, and Alice Pattie. *Up From Grief.* San Francisco: Harper and Row Publishers, Inc., 1969. Pp. 146.

Perkins, John M. *Let Justice Roll Down.* Ventura: Regal Books, 1976.

Tournier, Paul. *The Violence Within.* Trans. Edwin Hudson. New York: Harper and Row Publishers, 1978.